WORDS TO LOVE A PLANET

*An Illustrated Dictionary of
Language, Landscape and Life*

ELLA FRANCES SANDERS

Michael O'Mara Books Limited

Also by Ella Frances Sanders

*Lost in Translation: An Illustrated Compendium of
Untranslatable Words from Around the World*

*The Illustrated Book of Sayings: Curious
Expressions from Around the World*

Eating the Sun: Small Musings on a Vast Universe

Close Again

*Everything, Beautiful: A Guide to Finding
Hidden Beauty in the World*

Contents

Introduction v

Seasons 1

Land 37

Time 73

Water 101

Weather 135

Home 165

Being 191

Acknowledgements 227
Index of Terms 228
About the Author 231

'Do we want a language to build us a prison,
or do we want language to build us a home?'

– Amanda Leduc, 'It's Just a Figure of Speech'
(*from* Tongues: On Longing and Belonging through Language)

Introduction

Within the time I needed to write and illustrate this book countless unseen stars have stretched themselves thin, miles of delicate coastline have eroded into our oceans, millions of people have died of natural or unnatural causes, and my own feelings about everything have circled, and circled, and circled. Wolves softly but persistently padding around objects of interest, or of distrust. I have circled in despairing and delighted ways, spiraled because it is human to spiral, and asked the freshly stitched truths to stay close. Time will go on without us, but we are running out of it, and this left me quite unable to do anything except put these planetary words down on paper.

Over ten years after the publication of my first book,* I find myself drawn more than ever, mothlike, to languages and their ability to help us believe, or not believe, in reality, the ability of language to write or suggest stories we had never thought to read before. My belief is that one can never read too much when it comes to narratives that invite something better to sit at the table, though the language I currently read in and my native tongue, English, is a language that has historically erased others, violently, a colonizing language soaked through with oppression, and so that this book has been researched and written in such a language is not lost on me – for a while I did not believe I was a person who should carry out this collecting, but as I have said, we are running out of time.

What I came to think is this: Although I am someone who naturally feels most at home living within the silent paying of close attention, someone rightfully hesitant to fill too much more space with a language already far too pervasive and loud, there would nevertheless be words within my own reach and within other languages that, if collected together and explained, might help

---

* *Lost in Translation: An Illustrated Compendium of Untranslatable Words from Around the World* (Ten Speed Press, 2014).

people better love and care for their surrounding environments, their fragile ecosystems, themselves, others, anything.

That it might help to print in four-colour ink something that sets out to say, *You are allowed to want this to be different; you are allowed to call things by their other ancient names; you are allowed to want all this to be more beautiful.* At the very least, I wanted to give people pause for thought and, at the very best, expand people enough to actively demand or take part in the mending of damage. There exists a UN report noting that one language disappears from the face of the Earth every two weeks, a fact that has haunted me ever since first reading – I wonder how many vocabularies now lost to the accelerating drink of power and oppression contained words and knowledge that would have helped us better serve this ailing planet of ours.

The earthly environments, both near and far, that could have, once upon an epoch, easefully sustained every last species have now been drastically altered, damaged, and desiccated, and so it is no wonder that descriptions and definitions within widely spoken languages needed to change too, and grow, adapting as they tend to do in the face of mutation and modern technologies. The stories and the knowledge that might have helped and encouraged more of us to love this planet, to better know and understand ourselves as custodians rather than as occupiers, those threads have been there all along within Indigenous cultures but were intentionally buried by colonialism and violence, and it feels important to acknowledge that regardless of what the finite space of this book has or has not provided for, there are entire worlds of sacred comprehending that deserve to be recognized and respected.

The hope is quite simple: Give someone words for the natural things usually left unnoticed, dismissed, or passed by, and that same someone will grow to feel strongly enough to want to protect them. Not to have control over them but to realize there is a dignity to be found in the attentive preservation and nourishing of living systems, whether the ruling powers that be realize this or not. One of many hopes to spiral around in the months and years to come.

Our tiny experiences on this small cosmic speck are all carried out, recorded, in some kind of language, verbal or non-verbal, a language spoken by one or by millions, recorded only in memory or in images or on paper – it would be rare now for anyone to slip through the net of visible belonging in this way. It makes a great deal of sense, then, that more people are reaching out toward different, more diverse ways of describing and translating both their experiences and environments during what are for most of us incredibly troubled and confusing rotations of our one and only world. To better understand ourselves in the present moment, to imagine a gentler future, is to need different ways to say aloud the things we know, feel and see to be true.

One of the more meaningful definitions of translation I've encountered framed the process not as one of moving words between languages but rather of migrating understanding or meaning across distances, and it seems both reasonable and right that the fullest, most vivid meaning of a word can only truly be understood by someone if the language in question belongs to them. We can close gaps a little, maybe even a lot, meet each other's eyes in an approximation of knowing or empathy but we can never close those gaps completely, and I don't think we need to try to. What seems to me most essential is to make room in your life for other ways of being, room for people to be other ways around you, room for other ways to look at the living things already existing closest to you while helping those who exist at a distance. To consider, however briefly or thoroughly you would like to, your own life, your own lived landscapes, and the ways in which you are going about loving both people and planet.

A Note on Formatting & Pronunciation

Throughout this book the words offered are - on their first appearance and when written using the Latin alphabet - formatted in italics regardless of language, not to earmark them as foreign but simply in order that a reader might focus on them with more ease. In reality, and everywhere, different languages are spoken fluidly and interchangeably within families, within communities - rhythms, meanings and memories swim indistinct and harmonious regardless of their language of origin, regardless of what, in written texts, might be italicized or put in quotation marks.

Pronunciations are included throughout, not using the IPA (International Phonetic Alphabet) but spelled out phonetically to ensure that as many readers as possible can get a sense of how these words sound when said aloud, with stressed syllables capitalized if relevant. With many languages containing sounds non-existent in English, this means the pronunciations are therefore approximate.

Seasons

Or: *It's always changing,
and this is a reason to look up*

I f there is one thing that has held me to the fact of this Earth more than anything else, it is seasons. The life and death of them, the inescapable ephemerality and blink-and-you-miss-it of them, the awareness they can lend to one's physical presence on this planet – if you care to notice. The majority of my own life has been lived in the Northern Hemisphere, places ranging within their seasons from hoarfrosts to heat waves, and as such it is difficult to imagine a personal reality in which the seasonal changes are any less marked. The trees are dense green, then they are skeletal waiting. There are birds building nests above my door, then they leave.

I spend winters feeling perpetually cold, summers forgetting how to be warm, and the seasons in between pass too quickly if I let them. How to not let them pass too quickly: Watch extra closely during the weeks when leaves first appear in tender greens on deciduous trees; that bulbs can wait invisible underground for months before appearing out of the pale blue of spring; you wake up one March day and everything feels vital again; the first day of a year when the sunlight actually warms the body; early blossoms too quickly falling to carpet ambivalent concrete; the exact hour when the first swift returns from Africa; house martins flying back and forth between the mud of the river edge and the nook above the front door to build a nest together; finally enough heat that swimming in the loch-fed river appeals; more light in the evenings than one knows what to do with; the relief skin feels when exposed to morning sun; the possibility of leaving the doors and windows open all day; the inevitability of September; the first dusk of a year that somehow contains within it the precise scent of autumn; leaves falling in a way that suggests letting go is acceptable and indeed for the best; the first brief snow; ice-cold rain in the glow of streetlights; the freezing of outside water taps; birds gathering to feast on the red berries of holly and rowan; binoculars always in the bedroom window to look at migrating passersby; carpets of moss-nestled fungi in forests; the turning of Japanese maple leaves from a proud, rich burgundy to wet mulch; giving oneself up to the kind of deep frosts that never quite thaw completely from one day to the next; sting of woodsmoke; the quiet of a second snowfall; the turning of a year.

No matter where in the world a person lives, no matter how minimal or marked the seasonal changes in that place might be, we are powerfully bound as creatures to those shifts in ways that – aside from Indigenous knowledge – have, for the most part, been forgotten, dismissed. We don't know how to sense autumn storms anymore. We don't know how to smell soft rain coming or which trees hold on to their leaves the longest. We don't recognize sickness in plants or know the favoured nesting sites of certain birds. And for all that loss, we are diminished. It is like a dormancy of knowing, one that many people are seemingly more than happy to leave both buried and unacknowledged, one that leaves us far more vulnerable to the effects of a sticky-clawed, sick, profit-fueled society.

It is an untethering in that we are *supposed* to be tethered to the humming cycles of this planet; we are *supposed* to adjust our living around them, abide by their ebbs and flows. The Western (read: colonialist, capitalist) notion of growth is certainly not growth as nature would recognize it, and because we are biologically within rather than set apart from all that is natural, we, too, are meant to grow in animal ways and at animal speeds, not machine ones. The speeds at which most people – most continents – now move and build and damage and pollute would feel to the seasons as breakneck ones, a blur of destruction and disrepair. Even our use of the term 'the natural world' provides a degree of apartness, because although humans have certainly created a very *unnatural* world, at the end of a day – at the end of a season, a year, a life – it is just *the world*. There is only one, and the persistent, unconscious need to frame it as something separate further depresses that dormancy of knowing.

There are so many histories, or people, or corporations that could be blamed, but I don't believe there is time for blame anymore – differentiating of course between blame and accountability. We need, desperately, to unfurl from its sleep our knowledge and understanding of seasonal rhythms before it is too late – before we are instead waking up to birdless mornings and silent, dead forests. It is already happening. We are supposed to be reading the seasons in the same way we read books.

The seasonal words forming the following chapter are about relating to seasons in ways that might not have occurred before: words to know winter better, words to know summer from more of its sides, words to encourage the paying of attention to small shifts in surroundings. Words that help to both hear and see the symphonies of spring and autumn. Words to provide small maps to things that at one time were wordless – we need the words now; too long has passed since we knew the seasons without speaking. Because to isolate ourselves from these shifts, to numb ourselves to them, is to make us less human, less expansive, less so many of the things we need in order to mend.

As the seasons across the planet are becoming more and more misshapen, it is crucial that in our own places, around our own homes, we learn how to recognize the shape of nature's normality, of balance, of things falling into sequence as they are meant to. Where I live, the cherry trees should not be blossoming in January, but last year they did, and thousands of migrating pink-footed geese should have filled the farmlands, but they didn't. It is unnerving to notice a season out of balance, and noticing for most of us is formed from a combination of two things: language and attention. We are supposed to be listening, and feeling, and knowing, and waiting patiently, slowly, for the return of spring.

apricity
noun
English
ah-PRIS-i-tee

Meaning warmth or light from the sun. From the Latin *apricitās* and *aprīcus*, the latter of which in Medieval Latin had the meaning of delectable or delightful.

To *apricate*, as a verb, is to bask in the sun: *aprication*, *apricating*.

solvegg
noun
Norwegian
SOOL-vegg

Literally meaning 'sun wall' or 'solar wall,' with *i solveggen* translating as 'by the wall of sun.' Being able to find a sunny, south-facing wall or corner, even on cold days, where one can enjoy the warming rays.

Wari

noun
Pitjantjatjara
wah-RREE

The A<u>n</u>angu are Aboriginal people of the Central Australian desert,* near the sacred sandstone giant ofUlu<u>r</u>u, and mainly speak the dialects of Pitjantjatjara and Yankunytjatjara, which, when written, use fourteen letters of the English alphabet, along with the extra mark of an underline beneath some letters to indicate a retroflex (a consonant sound produced by the tongue being curled upward and backward).

Indigenous A<u>n</u>angu seasons total five, and these include *Wari*, which spreads from late May into July. Wari is cold, when mornings are characterized by *nyinnga* (frost) and *kulyar-kulyarpa* (mist or dew) but not a lot of rain.

The other seasons are *Itjanu*, sporadic storms and fast-moving puffed clouds bringing rain (January through March); *Wanitjunkupai*, cold weather creeping over Ulu<u>r</u>u and clouds from the south sitting low without much rain (April and May); *Piriyakutu* (August to September), with *piriya* the name of the warm wind arriving from the northwest – this season is also characterized by animals breeding and food plants fruiting and flowering; and *Mai wiyaringkupai*, the hottest season, with its stormy skies, lightning, little rain and scarce food.

---

* In 1981, the Pitjantjatjara Land Rights Act was passed, which returned over 40,000 square miles of land to the A<u>n</u>angu.

उतु / utu
noun
Pāli, Sanskrit
OO-too

Pāli, a classical language of ancient India and the Theravāda Buddhist texts – related to Sanskrit though not directly descended – ceased to exist as a literary language in mainland India in the fourteenth century, continuing on elsewhere until the eighteenth.

The word *utu* refers to good or proper time, to time of a year, to seasons, and in these ancient texts, there are often just three seasons mentioned: the hot, rainy and wintry seasons.

But then, an example of how translation is less about moving precise meaning than it is about moving experience might be in how the same three letters happen to shape-shift: Utu in Swahili means humanity, or human nature; in Ternate it means harvest (secondarily a kind of small squid); in Finnish it describes haze or mist (see page 129). And in a few other languages (at least Buginese, Galoli and Tetum) it refers to a louse.

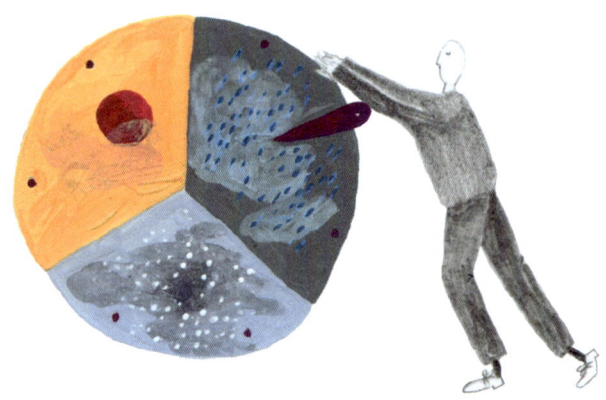

Zeitgeber
noun
German, New Coinage
ZITE-gee-ber

Literally translated to mean 'time-giver,' *Zeitgeber* was coined in the late 1950s by German physician Jürgen Aschoff, who pioneered research into chronobiology, or the study of biological rhythms. Zeitgeber refers to an environmental shift or cue that regulates an organism's circadian clock, ultimately regulating in time to Earth's great, ordinary rotation. The balance of daylight and darkness at certain times of the year that gently nudges bird populations into their inconceivable migrations, or changing tides, or shifting temperatures – all things as these are Zeitgebers.

uashtessiu
animate noun
Innu-aimun
ooack-TE-soo

Innu-aimun – literally translated as meaning 'language of the people,' sometimes called Montagnais as a residue from French colonization – is an endangered Indigenous language spoken in a variety of dialects by over 10,000 Innu in areas of both Labrador and Quebec, in the east of Canada. A feature of the language is the distinction of nouns as animate and inanimate, viewed as living and non-living, and, beautifully, the living includes not only people and animals but also trees, plants and anything else believed to possess animate qualities, like snowshoes or stones.

Uashtessiu is an animate noun and refers to vegetation lighting up in the colours of autumn, the turning yellow of leaves.

The Innu *pishimuat* (months) are named for environmental changes, creatures, time and temperatures: *Uashtessiu-pishimu*, the month of leaves turning yellow (October); *Shiship-pishimu*, the month of the waterfowl (April); *Ushkau-pishimu*, the month of new antlers (September); *Pishimuss*, the little month (December).

紅葉 / kōyō
noun
Japanese
koh-yo

Comprised of the characters 紅 (crimson) and 葉 (leaf), *kōyō* refers literally to the colourful autumn foliage but is also linked to the Japanese cultural tradition of going out to admire the astonishing autumnal changes of trees, 紅葉狩り (*momijigari*, literally meaning 'maple leaf hunting'), a practice of appreciation dating as far back as the Heian period, between 794 and 1185, initially a pastime available only to the wealthy and socially elite; in the Edo period (1603–1868) general travel and seasonal outings became much more widely accessible to far more people, with the practice of viewing and appreciating nature cementing itself more firmly as a tradition for everyone. A long time to have been appreciating autumn – imagine for a lengthy moment the near-infinite leaves that have budded and grown and fallen and decomposed in those 1,000 years since.

листопад / listopad
noun
Russian
lis-toh-PAD

Quite simply, the falling of leaves, which, to be more scientific, is known as the process of defoliation. *Listopad* is an archaic seasonal term for the month of October (or November, depending on region), or what looks most like October* in the Northern Hemisphere: the month of changing colours, falling leaves and the sugary scent of things beginning to break themselves all the way down. Now with solely poetic usage in modern Russian, found in literature and poetry to evoke slightly melancholic autumnal themes.

---

* In modern usage, листопад is the name for November in Ukrainian, Polish, Czech and Belarusian, with it uniquely referring to October in Croatian.

rummescent
noun
English, New Coinage
rum-MESS-sent

A neologism coined by Welsh philosopher Ginny Battson, *rummescent* describes the smell of leaf decay combined with early, misty mornings, rich soil, cooler evenings – the scent brought about by the annual fall of deciduous leaves.

Maeinschein
noun
German
MY-en-shine

Literally translates to 'may-shine,' and refers to the green-golden sunlight that finds its way through the fresh, supple leaves of May and early June.

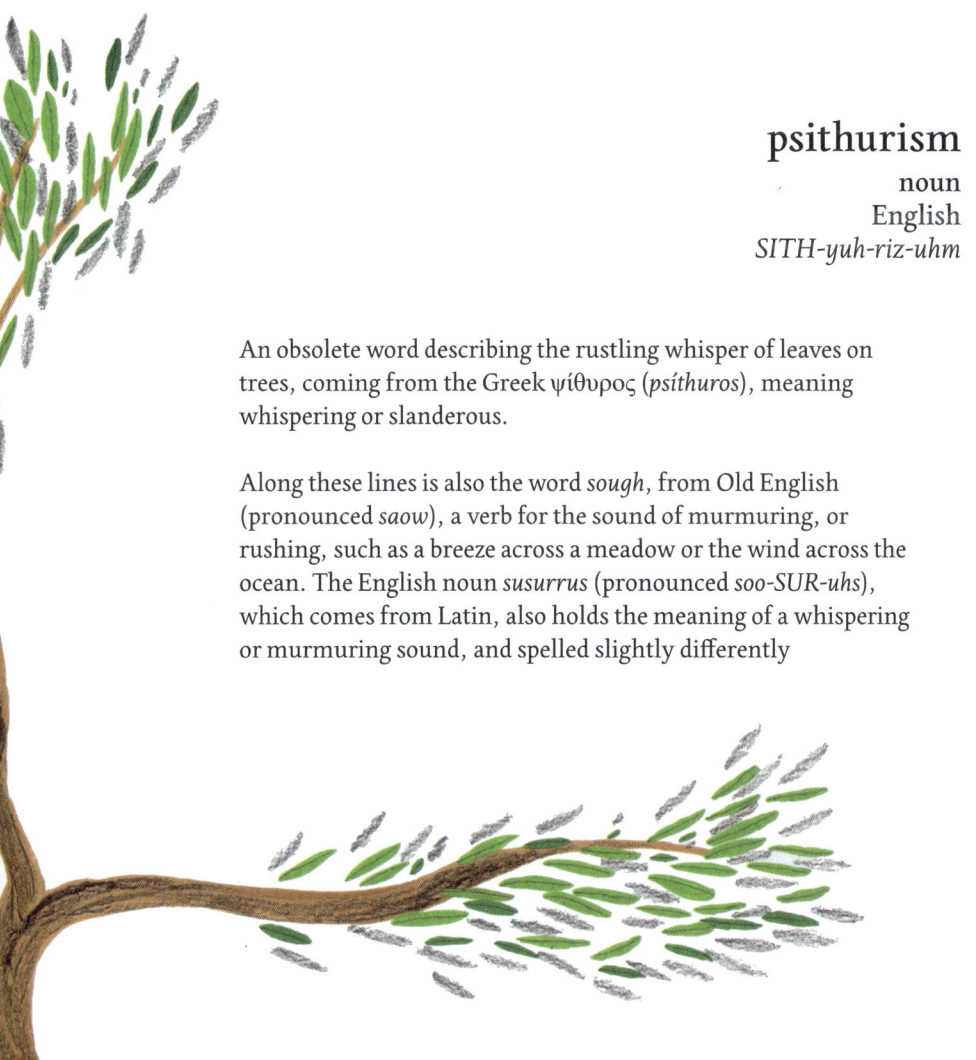

psithurism

noun
English
SITH-yuh-riz-uhm

An obsolete word describing the rustling whisper of leaves on trees, coming from the Greek ψίθυρος (*psíthuros*), meaning whispering or slanderous.

Along these lines is also the word *sough*, from Old English (pronounced *saow*), a verb for the sound of murmuring, or rushing, such as a breeze across a meadow or the wind across the ocean. The English noun *susurrus* (pronounced *soo-SUR-uhs*), which comes from Latin, also holds the meaning of a whispering or murmuring sound, and spelled slightly differently as *susurrous*, it becomes an adjective – something full of whispering, rustling sound. Both followed on from *susurration*, which describes a whispering sound, a murmur, something half indistinct, though the original fifteenth-century meaning was closer to describing malicious rumour.

花見 / hanami

noun
Japanese
han-a-mee

The Japanese tradition of viewing tree blossoms, originally a viewing and appreciation of plum blossoms, though particularly now associated with those of 桜 (*sakura*), cherry trees, most commonly of ornamental types. Composed of the characters 花 (flower) and 見 (to look), *hanami* or *o-hanami* translates to mean 'flower viewing.'

Today, many millions of people visit Japan expressly to see sakura, a flocking made especially possible because the cherry trees are flowering at slightly different times of year depending on where they are in the country – though each tree holds on to its blossoms only for around two weeks.

A person wonders then what it might be like to show a similar degree of appreciation and reverence for the blossoms closer to home, as opposed to traveling great distances to look up at trees, which will likely not speak the same language we do. To hold conversations with the trees at arm's length seems the thing to do at this moment in time, when everything is fragile and so much is overlooked. The tree that stands closest to you – do you know what it is, what it whispers?

bon hiver
interjection
French
bon EE-ver

A French greeting and sentiment, traditionally used on the day of the first snow, literally means 'good winter,' with *hiver* also referring to the season itself.

frondescence

noun
English
fron-DES-sence

As a botanical noun, *frondescence* is the time at which a plant or tree unfurls its leaves, or a sometimes-used term for 'foliage.'

From the Latin *frondēscere*, meaning to put forth leaves, and *frōns*, meaning foliage. As the rare adjective *frondescent*, meaning a plant or tree producing leaves, also *frondiferous* meaning leaf-bearing and, lastly, *frondless*, a plant not having large leaves.

Also related and lovely is the word *vernation* (pronounced *ver-NAY-shun*), which refers either to the formation of new leaves in spring or the type of arrangement of leaves within a bud. Such arrangements as rolled lengthwise (circinate) or pleated lengthwise (plicate). In ferns, for example, vernation is circinate, all rolled up, as with a fiddlehead (so named after the scrolled shape at the top of a violin).

Vernation itself comes from the Latin *vernare*, to flourish, and *ver*, meaning spring.

вирій / výrij
noun
Ukrainian
VIH-ree

From Slavic mythology, вирій is a place where birds fly for the winter months but can also be used to describe a heavenly place. Similar in meaning to the Finnish *lintukoto*, which is also rooted in mythology.

aestivation

noun
English
ess-ti-VAY-shun

A kind of opposite to hibernation, *aestivation* is the state of animal dormancy that can occur in the summer, bringing a lowered metabolic rate and inactivity during hot, dry periods. Such as with some snails, who would otherwise dry out completely in more extreme summer conditions, aestivating by burrowing into mud and sealing up their shells until things ease.

A greater number of vertebrates aestivate compared to invertebrates. This long summer sleep is found in creatures like desert tortoises, crocodiles, salamanders and frogs. A few mammals are known to aestivate too: a type of dwarf lemur and East African hedgehogs.

Aestivate can also mean the act of, as a human, spending the summer in one place and forgoing any kind of travel – aestivation as the act of passing the summer. *Aestival* subsequently means typical of or pertaining to the months of summer.

Blueschtfährtli

noun
Swiss German
bloosht-FERT-li

A compound word made from the words for 'blossom' and 'little drive,' *Blueschtfährtli* refers to the May-time tradition of going for springtime drives with the sole purpose of appreciating the trees dressed in their flowering blooms.

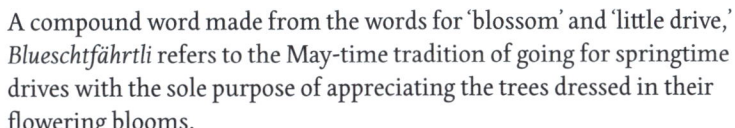

候 / kō

noun
Japanese
koh

Kō, meaning 'season' or 'climate condition,' sits within 七十二候 (*shichijūni-kō*), which are the seventy-two miniature seasons throughout a year, an ancient Japanese almanac of small seasonal shifts and the opportunity to notice and appreciate them. Within this calendar, there are the same four seasons many would recognize and know, but within each of those four are six parts – each lasting about fifteen days – along with three even smaller divisions within each lasting around five days. Derived from the Chinese lunisolar calendar, which takes into account both the moon's orbit of the Earth and Earth's orbit of the sun, it was adjusted for the Japanese climatic changes in 1685 by Shibukawa Shunkai, an official astronomer of the Edo period.

Within *haru* (春, spring) are tiny seasons, like 'fish swim after the thaw' (魚上氷, 14–18 February), 'sparrows build the first nest' (雀始巣, 21–25 March), and 'last frost, rice seedlings grow' (霜止出苗, 25–29 April).

Natsu (夏, summer) includes the microseasons 'worms surface' (蚯蚓出, 10–14 May), 'plums ripen to yellow' (梅子黄, 16–20 June), 'first lotus blossoms' (蓮始開, 12–16 July), and 'heavy rain falls from time to time' (大雨時行, 3–7 August).

Aki (秋, autumn) will find you with 'evening cicadas sing' (寒蝉鳴, 13–17 August), 'swallows leave' (玄鳥去, 18–22 September), and 'light rains sometimes fall' (霎時施, 28 October–1 November).

Finally, *fuyu* (冬, winter) brings along with it 'land starts to freeze' (地始凍, 12–16 November), 'salmon gather and swim upstream' (鱖魚群, 17–21 December), 'wheat sprouts under snow' (雪下出麦, 1–4 January), and 'ice thickens on streams' (水沢腹堅, 25–29 January).

Influenced by weather changes, agricultural elements and ecological shifts, the natural cycles that try to continue year in and year out – despite our deep and troubling climatic interference – and often focusing on visual markers, auditory cues or tangible happenings in the environment, such small and beautiful seasons as shichijūni-kō provide an opportunity to adjust one's relationship with the passing of time, to notice, consider and appreciate the tiny, often fragile and yet instrumental changes within the land.

sōlstitium

noun
Latin
sol-STI-she-um

Sōlstitium refers to a standing still of the sun or the pausing of its motion, its solstice and additionally (though more obscurely) the long heat of summer. At the time of a solstice, the movement of the sun's path, as seen from Earth, will appear as a brief pause before a reversing in direction – a moment of standing still.

laethanta na riabhaí

noun
Irish
ley-HUN-tuh na REE-vee

From a tale in Irish (Gaeilge) folklore and translating literally – there are different dialectal spellings and pronunciations – as the 'brindled days,' though also known as the 'borrowing days,' *laethanta na riabhaí* references the first three days of April containing such awful weather that they appear to be borrowed from March, or the other way around.

The word *riabhach* means striped, or brindled, but can also mean drab, or dull, with *lá riabhach* referring to a particularly dull day.

新緑 / shinryoku
noun
Japanese
shin-ryoh-koo

Following the cherry blossom season in Japan – which traditionally falls in late March or early April depending on the region – comes the first brightly fresh green of the year, *shinryoku*. Normally arriving with May, sometimes a little earlier in April, though possibly as late as June, after the last blossoms have fallen but before the onset of true summer, with the entire month of May being the most strongly associated culturally with shinryoku.

Formed from the characters 新 (new) and 緑 (green), shinryoku also carries associations with the first rice planting, with the convergence of these two things holding spiritual and hopeful significance for growth and the future.

森林浴 / shinrin-yoku

noun
Japanese, New Coinage
shin-rin-yoh-koo

With greenness of leaf comes a fullness of forest, and Japanese culture has long held and maintained a practice of spending time in such environments. The term *shinrin-yoku* (*shinrin** meaning forest, and *yoku* meaning bath, or bathing) was coined in 1982 by the Japanese Ministry of Agriculture, Forestry and Fisheries as part of an initiative to help alleviate high levels of mental and physical stress within the population, and to more directly research and emphasize the benefits of spending time in nature.

With two-thirds of the country swaddled in forest, it is perhaps unsurprising that a precise term shaped itself to the practice of what is, simply and without any embellishment or explanation, spending time with trees.

While this particular Japanese term has gained appeal in recent decades – spreading in a manner not unlike that of windborne seeds – it has been generally, planetarily known since antiquity that there are benefits to absorbing the exhales of a forest, and in the Middle Ages, phytochemicals were already being used to treat certain diseases. Finland is also a country (the most forested in Europe) that has, since the nineteenth century, been notably aware of the benefits trees provide us mortals. We are made calmer by trees, less anxious in their presence, our parasympathetic nervous systems quietening down.

We should never have required additional or researched reasons to revere our forests, and their protection should have always been implicit, recognized – what grows in fifty or a hundred years can, most horrifically, be sliced down in seconds.

---

* Japanese has several words for 'forest,' depending on the landscape in question. 林 (*hayashi*) refers to a forest that is more manmade than wild, 森 (*mori*) is used when speaking about areas of extensive wild forest, and 森林 (*shinrin*) comes with a connotation of a particularly tall and ancient forest.

marcescence

noun
Latin
mar-SESS-ence

The Latin *marcescere* means to fade, or wither, and is where *marcescence* comes from, which refers to the holding and waiting of dead leaves on trees during the winter months – seen most noticeably on species like beech and oak. Tenuously attached, and usually only eventually dislodged by high winds or new leaf growth.

The reasons for this are not completely clear or decided upon, but wondered to be things like protection for new buds, shelter for birds, or keeping hold of leaves until spring when they can fall around the base of a tree and become beneficial mulch.

துளிர் / tuḷir

noun
Tamil
TOO-lirr

Technically meaning a bud, or a smallest new leaf, but can also mean to thrive, typically if something started from scratch or started small. In Tamil, there is also அரும்பு (*arumpu*, pronounced *ah-RHUM-boo*), which refers specifically to a flower or leaf bud in the moment just before opening up to the sun, halfway between states.

風物詩 / fūbutsushi

noun
Japanese
foo-buh-tsu-shee

Fūbutsushi are culturally familiar and symbolic scenes, markers, activities or traditions within a particular season that capture that season's spirit – the word 季節感 (*kisetsukan*) would refer to a sense of the seasons and their changes. Fūbutsushi can bring about anticipatory feelings, or nostalgic ones directed toward the past, and literally translated means 'a poem of seasonal things,' though in modern Japanese it most commonly references hallmarks of a season, such as snow in the winter or school ceremonies in spring.

Meanwhile, 個人的な懐かしさ (*kojinteki na natsukashisa*) would reference more personal nostalgias: the first damp sweetness of rotting leaves, the smell of a soap used only during childhood summers, the sight of a split fruit on the sidewalk, the sting of woodsmoke in the nose.

wintercearig
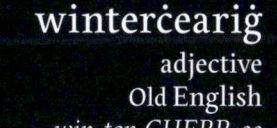
adjective
Old English
win-ter-CHERR-ee

Literally 'winter-cares' and meaning something like winter sorrows or winter sadness: a sorrowful feeling brought about by the cold, still, dark nature of winter.

takatalvi

noun
Finnish
tukka-TUHL-vi

Literally translating to 'behind-winter,' *takatalvi* is a return of winter while technically within the season of spring: a small second winter often bringing with it a snowfall.

یلدا / yaldâ

noun
Farsi
YAL-dah

Borrowed from the Syriac word *yaldā*, in Farsi *yaldâ* is the word for the winter solstice, the darkest and longest night, meaning 'rebirth' and referring to the sun's returning with the light. It also refers to the Iranian festival شب یلدا (Šab-e Yaldâ, or Yalda Night), held to celebrate that longest, darkest night, following on from which the nights shorten and the light lengthens – celebrated, too, in Afghanistan, Azerbaijan and Iraqi Kurdistan, among others. (Farsi as a language is known in Afghanistan as Dari and as Tajik in Tajikistan.)

In ancient Persia, *yaldâ* festivities were centered on an evergreen tree, with wishes being wrapped in silk cloths and hung on the branches.

kaamos

noun
Finnish
KAH-mohs

Kaamos means 'polar night' and refers to the period of time between late November and early February when the sun simply doesn't rise over the horizon in places north of the Arctic Circle and south of the Antarctic one – in the north of Finland this can be up to fifty-two days.

It can also mean general gloominess of weather during autumn and winter, or even the moods that for some people accompany such times. The word kaamos comes from the Sámi *skábma*, which is itself of Scandinavian origin; the present-day Norwegian equivalent to kaamos is *skamtid*, which translates as short, or bleak time (*skam* means short).

Land

Or: *Our relationship with it,
and how we move through*

Today, without much exception, people know the landscapes and environments we live within and alongside do not look as they should. Everything that could possibly have been taken from them has been taken, everything that could feasibly have been cut down has been cut, all that could be mined has been violently carved out, and any geographical features relatively out of eyesight have been filled or covered or soaked in plastic. Our innate relationships – having evolved over millennia – with what were once rich habitats teeming with health and complexity have been discouraged, turned away, fenced off or removed altogether. We now mostly regard those habitats through closed windows held in place by polyvinyl chloride frames. I think we have paid an inordinately high price for this, and that price seems, most unnervingly, to be the more tender half of our humanity, the most empathetic and generous aspects.

  This geographical severing has long been completely out of the control of the everyday surviving person, often strategically out of earshot and eyeline, implemented and then dangerously embraced by the smiling political and corporate figures who seem unable to think beyond the timescale of a distended personal bank account. Repeatedly, and for centuries, the wealth of a relative handful has been placed above the healthful functioning of lung-like ecosystems – time and time again, the ecological consequences dismissed, downplayed or denied. There is no transplant available for a planet. The most beautiful and biodiverse of landscapes have been taken from you and damaged, and those who have inflicted the damage now shrug, deny or scuttle away to hide within their nests of billions.

For most of this time, it was not possible to put precise words to the violence, either because the fallout of fossil fuels wasn't as publicly known about or simply because the language being spoken and the books being written did not yet contain the terms that could define and, therefore, raise awareness for these new destructions. So people have coined them: ecocide, solastalgia, nanoplastics, forever chemicals.

There have always been spoken languages woven together with terms that acknowledge the importance of a person's connection to land, the conservation of land, that name and note precise features and interactions and minutiae, that honour the delicate, furious balance nature needs to maintain within itself. As those words of connection were forgotten, banned and buried, the feeling of being in harmony with nature subsided along with them, replaced by bulldozers and cinder blocks and boreholes, and 4,000 years after it is believed humans first used coal as a fuel, this Earth's convulsions of pain couldn't be plainer to see. Most of us didn't know the old words that spoke of connection and care and reverence were even there, but that doesn't mean our bodies don't remember.

It is a truth universally acknowledged that men named all of the things, a naming carried out in conjunction with an infantile traipsing about the planet, declaring ownership and occupation of that which was already cared for by others and already called by another name in another tongue. Centuries-long attempts to smother the ancient linguistic origins and deep Indigenous understanding of so many places with violence, with industry and power, with ever more violence. And they are still naming ever more things. Present-day populations in most large societies have been trained to believe that anything with an amount of perceived importance must be given names, titles, declarations, branding. Supposed societal importance or worthiness is still conferred with titles; the nameless have always been omitted from history. If something doesn't have a name, a word, a marker of some sort, then most people do not think to go looking for it, let alone care about or protect it. The modern logic is as follows: If the way certain branches lean and tenderly touch the river surface is nameless, there is surely no reasonable impediment when it comes to the wielding of a chainsaw, the poisoning of an entire waterway.

So here follow some words for the land, to better know and understand it, to better recognize its nuance, to better protect it from further damage – it has suffered more than should ever have been plausible. There are words that equate to noticing the night sky differently, some words that return you to the trees, some that encourage noticing yourself out within landscapes as exactly that: as being *within* them rather than as a disconnected or disinterested passerby on the way to another digital screen. People say, when they know a place well, that they know it like the backs of their hands, but I scarcely think this happens anymore, and I don't think many would necessarily even recognize their own hands at all, places or no places. Instead, it might be that we need to relearn landscape, deeply, and that out of that learning, we will be able to better recognize our own hands, our own bodies, returned as they are to their true and natural backgrounds.

yillal

noun
Guugu Yimithirr
YILL-al

Also rendered Guugu Yimidhirr, Guguyimidjir, or various other spellings, Guugu Yimithirr is the language of the Indigenous Guugu Yimithirr people of Far North Queensland.

A *yillal* is a path across land or sky, recorded in song, dance, paintings and stories, that follows and marks a route taken by creator-beings. What is most beautiful and interesting about such paths is imagining them knowing Guugu Yimithirr does not have words for left or right, and instead, all instances where one might use either are replaced by directions of *gungga*, *jiba*, *naga* and *guwa*, similar in meaning to north, south, east and west. *Naga* meaning 'a small way east,' *nagaar* 'a little farther to the east,' and *nagaalu* meaning 'a long way east.'

This way of relating to the world and direction also reflects how the Guugu Yimithirr view themselves within the world: as while the majority of languages are highly egocentric in their explanation of direction – when we describe or encounter things as left or right those things are constantly changing as we ourselves alter in position – in Guugu Yimithirr, the language is positioning the speaker as near irrelevant in relation to things, the existence of a person merely thin air around and through which the world moves.

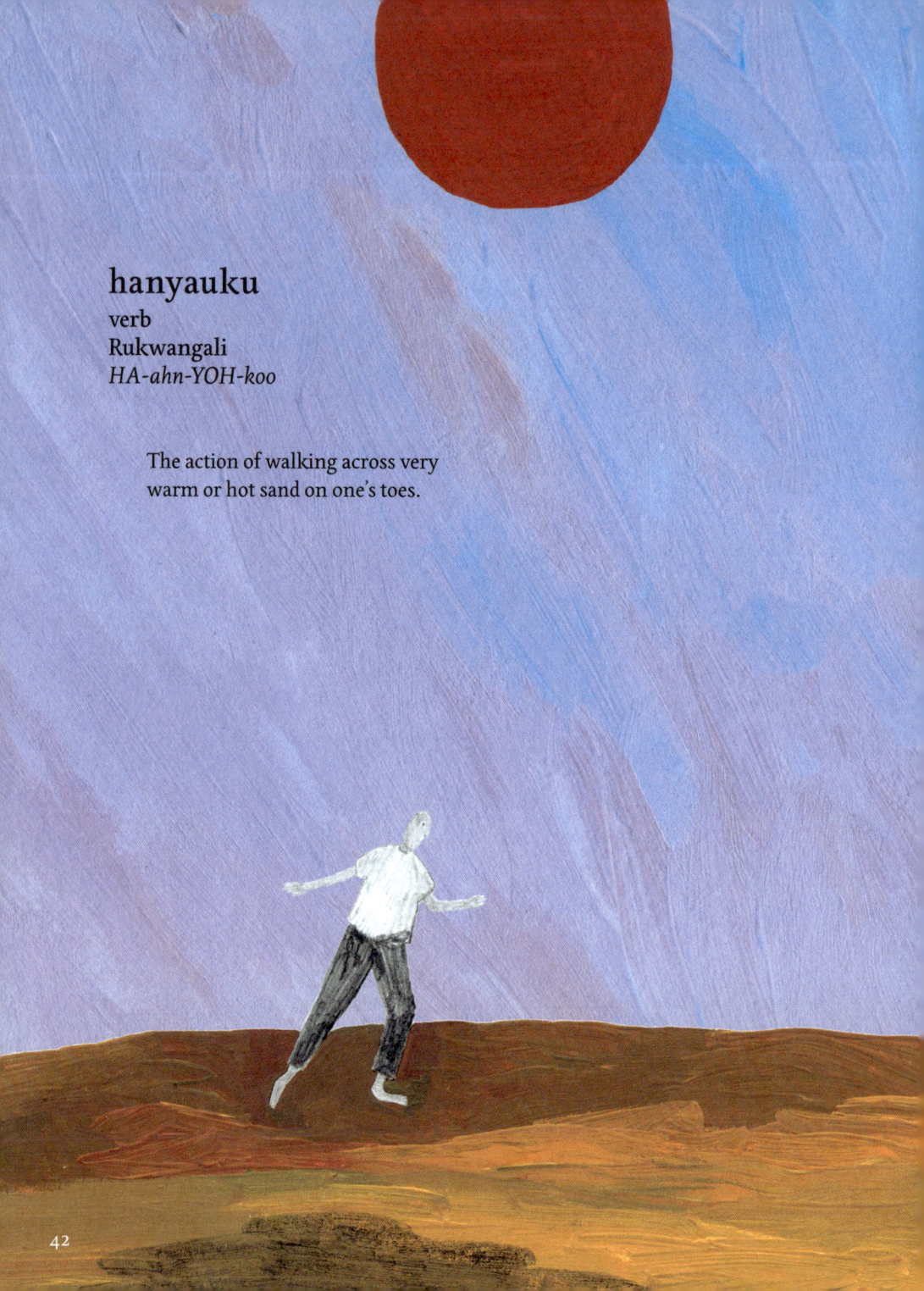

hanyauku
verb
Rukwangali
HA-ahn-YOH-koo

The action of walking across very warm or hot sand on one's toes.

不均斉 / fukinsei

noun
Japanese
foo-keen-sei

A natural, or spontaneous, balanced asymmetry, and within Japanese aesthetics referencing the idea that an intentional or accidental imbalance can be more beautiful than an enforced symmetry. Imperfection as an inherent part of existence, and beauty in the unbalanced, the lopsided and the irregular, with nature and its harmonious balanced-imbalances being an epitome of *fukinsei* in many ways.

snicket

noun
English, Northern
SNI-kit

Snicket is a word describing – frequently, though not exclusively – a path or passage or public right of way, often grassy underfoot, or slightly overgrown. Between things, between places, a pathway or secret that serves as a shortcut or back route from one place to another.

Less well known is *ginnel*, which describes a narrow passageway between or through buildings, such as a fenced or walled alleyway.

ritornello

noun
Italian
RREE-tor-NELL-oh

Translating as 'little return,' in music a *ritornello* refers to a recurring passage, while prior to the 1600s it was used more as an instruction to repeat a section of music.

I would like to propose a secondary, ordinary use of ritornello to mean the small returns we make countless times a day, a week, a life, to the things that are most essential to our living. For example, making a ritornello to the kitchen multiple times throughout a day in order to make tea, or a ritornello down the road to the mailbox, or a ritornello made by a bird to a particular spot in the garden. This life is built from millions of little returns.

skovstilhed

noun
Norwegian, New Coinage
SKOOV-stihl-hed

Seemingly absorbed and extrapolated from a piece of music by Norwegian composer Edvard Grieg (1843–1907) titled 'Skovstilhed,' op. 71, no. 4, and translated in various places as 'woodland peace' or 'peace of the woods' – *stilhed* meaning silence. *Skovstilhed* has been supposed to refer to the feeling produced by spending time among quiet trees, a kind of forest tranquility.

Related and lovely: The Welsh phrase *dod yn ôl at fy nghoed* (pronounced *DOHD un ohl at foh NGHOYD*), which literally means 'to return to my trees,' is used to mean the returning of oneself to a balanced state of mind.

montivagant

adjective, noun
English
mon-TI-vuh-gant

Seemingly used only during the middle of the 1600s as an adjective to describe wandering over mountains and hills, or as a noun to describe a person doing such wandering.

A relative of *noctivagant* (wandering about at night), *nubivagant* (moving throughout or among clouds), *omnivagant* (wandering generally everywhere), *nemorivagant* (wandering through forest and woodland), and even *extravagant*, which etymologically comes from a place of meaning to wander outside or beyond. All these *-vagants* arriving from the Latin word *vagari*, meaning 'wander.'

fjellvant
adjective
Norwegian
fee-YELL-vonte

Describes being accustomed to, or familiar with, walking in the mountains.

Bergdenken
noun
German
BAIRG-den-ken

Literally translates as 'mountain thinking' and refers to the longing to be among mountains, to be spending time in them.

huya ania

noun
Yaqui
hoo-yuh ah-ni-uh

Huya ania describes the 'wilderness world,' one of nine or more different worlds recognized by the Indigenous Yaqui people of Mexico and Arizona – locally the language is known as Yoeme or Yoem Noki – with many Yaqui believing that the Earth exists composed of many overlapping but distinct worlds, *aniam*. These include the *sea ania* (flower world), *tenku ania* (dream world), *tuka ania* (night world), *vawe ania* (world under the water), *kawi ania* (mountain world), and *yo ania* (enchanted world).

Each ania has its own qualities and forces; for example, the huya ania is a world where plants, animals and rocks are inherently one and communicate as one. Consequently, walking out in lands is a far more spiritual consideration, and as such, Yaqui would ask permission to approach and walk through the huya ania.

passeggiata

noun
Italian
pass-eh-JAHR-tuh

Coming from the verb *passeggiare,* which means to walk, a *passeggiata* is the quintessential Italian pastime of taking a leisurely walk with the purpose of simply strolling, socializing, people watching and world observing – traditionally an evening stroll taken in a town's central piazza. During the week, a passeggiata might be taken in the evening hours, and on the weekend at any hour.

βόλτα / vólta
noun
Greek
VOHL-tuh

Similar to the Italian passeggiata, a *βόλτα* is a leisurely walk, one most frequently shared with friends or family in the cooler evening hours. The common expression *πάμε βόλτα* (*páme vólta*) means 'let's take a turn' and is used often by Greeks when they are proposing to take a walk, a drive or just stretch out the legs.

This concept of an evening stroll is also expressed in Serbian, Czech and Slovak with the word *korzo*, while the Scots word *stravaig* refers to someone (a *stravaiger*) going for a stroll but in a rather more aimless and wandering way.

uitwaaien
verb
Dutch
OUT-vai-en

A compound word formed from *uit* (out) and *waaien* (to blow, of the wind). *Uitwaaien* (literally 'out-blowing') is the Dutch practice of going outside – the windier the weather, the better – to freshen one's mind, clear out stagnant stress and generally feel invigorated, such as becomes very necessary after a long day of sitting down inside.

Folded into the culture with its current definition since the early twentieth century and consequently not viewed as anything remarkable or out of the ordinary by those living in the Netherlands, any time you are feeling depleted of energy, stale, it is simply normal to go uitwaaien.

Another uniquely Dutch way of being outside is *dauwtrappen*, or 'dew-treading,' which refers to going outside while the grass is still covered in morning dew.

lieko

noun
Finnish
LEER-koh

Lieko refers to a fallen, rotting tree, particularly if the tree in question is at the bottom of a lake. Finnish does not stop there with precise tree descriptions: *kelo* (dead tree still standing, usually only the trunk but no bark); *konkelo* (dead tree, fallen but still leaning on something); *pökkelö* (dead tree standing but with only the outer bark layers remaining); *aihki* (a large coniferous tree); *petäjä* (old lone pine tree); *honka* (old pine tree with a straight trunk).

viridatas

noun
Latin
wier-RI-di-tas

A likely merging of the Latin words for 'green' and 'truth,' *viriditas* can literally mean 'growth,' or 'green,' an intense greenness, but also metaphorically vitality, vigour and verdure. Its theological usage is acknowledged widely to have been coined by Hildegard of Bingen (1098–1179), who saw viriditas as something to be cultivated both in and outside the body, a greening from within, the divineness of nature as a whole, and perhaps something we might now call photosynthesis. In her illustrated work *Scivias* (1151–1152), she alluded most succinctly to the oneness of everything: 'You understand so little of what is around you because you do not use what is within you.'*

* Hildegard of Bingen, *Scivias*, 1.2.29. Translation from Avis Clendenen, 'Hildegard: 'Trumpet of God' and 'Living Light,'' *Chicago Theological Seminary Register* 89, no. 2 (1999): 25.

desir

noun
Bahasa Indonesia
dess-SYER

Translated literally as 'whistle,' *desir* refers to the gentle sound of something, such as wind (*desir angin*) moving sand across a surface or dry leaves being moved along a roadside, or to describe the soft sound of waves (*desir ombak*).

Bahasa Indonesia ('language of Indonesia') is a standardized version of its ancestor Malay, and the intention behind this standardization was to make communication across the sprawling, vast Indonesian archipelago and its hundreds of regional languages, dialects and ethnic groups simpler and more inclusive – while it is technically the nation's official language, learned in schools and used in political discourse, its normative form is rarely used in everyday conversations, not only because it stifled other forms of cultural expression during the Suharto dictatorship and that feeling lingers, but also because it is most often being merged with other languages, such as Javanese or Balinese, along with countless small variations of slang, of local vernacular.

kertik

noun
Malay
KERR-tek

The sound made by dry leaves and twigs underfoot while walking.

mäntykangas

noun
Finnish
MAHN-too-kung-os

A *mäntykangas* refers to a variety of boreal forest containing mostly pine trees on a type of sandy ground. *Mänty* used to refer to a young pine tree, with words such as *petäjä* and *honka* referring to older pines depending on their characteristics; now mänty is used more generally to mean pine tree. *Kangas* means both fabric and a dry woodland area, and it is nice to think of mäntykangas as a kind of Earth-protecting cloth woven from trees.

celístia

noun
Catalan
sel-LIS-ti-uh

A word for the brightness emitted by stars, akin to starshine, or starlight. Perhaps from the Latin *caelestia*, meaning celestial things. Our night-sky stars are so far away and so comparatively cold that they cannot provide us with any actual light – brightness being different from inherent luminosity – and yet we have been mesmerized by them for as long as people have been people.

کهکشان / kahkašân

noun
Farsi
KAH-kah-shawn

Meaning galaxy, or the Milky Way (also holding the same meaning in both Dari and Tajik), *kahkašân* is formed of کاه (*kâh*, meaning straw, or hay) and کش (*keš*, meaning pull), with a suffix denoting a likeness, said to be because of the way the night-sky Milky Way resembles a road covered in a scattering of straw – as a word it holds within connotations of awe, wonder and the divine.

In many languages written using Arabic script, often only the consonants are represented, and unless represented by additional glyphs, the vowel sounds are then filled in when speaking – this is a type of alphabet called an abjad. The Persian alphabet, used to write Farsi, adds four letters to the Arabic one (پ چ ژ گ), giving it thirty-two letters in total.

воля / volia

noun
Ukrainian
VOHL-yuh

Often translated as 'freedom' in English but the complexities of the word run far deeper, its meaning within the country essential to its collective being. воля (*volia*) is a freedom without restriction: to live on one's native land, to speak one's own languages, the unquestionable right to self-determination. Secondarily translated as an inner strength, intention or willpower, воля is a kind of core resilience and philosophy knitting together the Ukrainian people – the courage to act, to stand up to the ongoing oppressive, silencing forces.

smultronställe

noun
Swedish
SMOOL-tron-STEL-eh

Literally translating as a 'wild strawberry spot,' in current usage *smultronställe* figuratively refers to a place where one has a feeling of safety, secreted away from things. Somewhere that contains refuge and solace, a cherished, discovered place with a sentimentality that you do not necessarily share with anyone else – smultronställe can also refer to a period of time when one felt this way.

Before its usage expanded, smultronställe meant more simply and literally a place where wild strawberries could be found and picked (and kept secret, much like people's favoured mushroom spots), or a place where one could go and sit among them in sun and just exist, and it can still be used to refer literally to a place where *smultrons* (strawberries) grow in abundance.

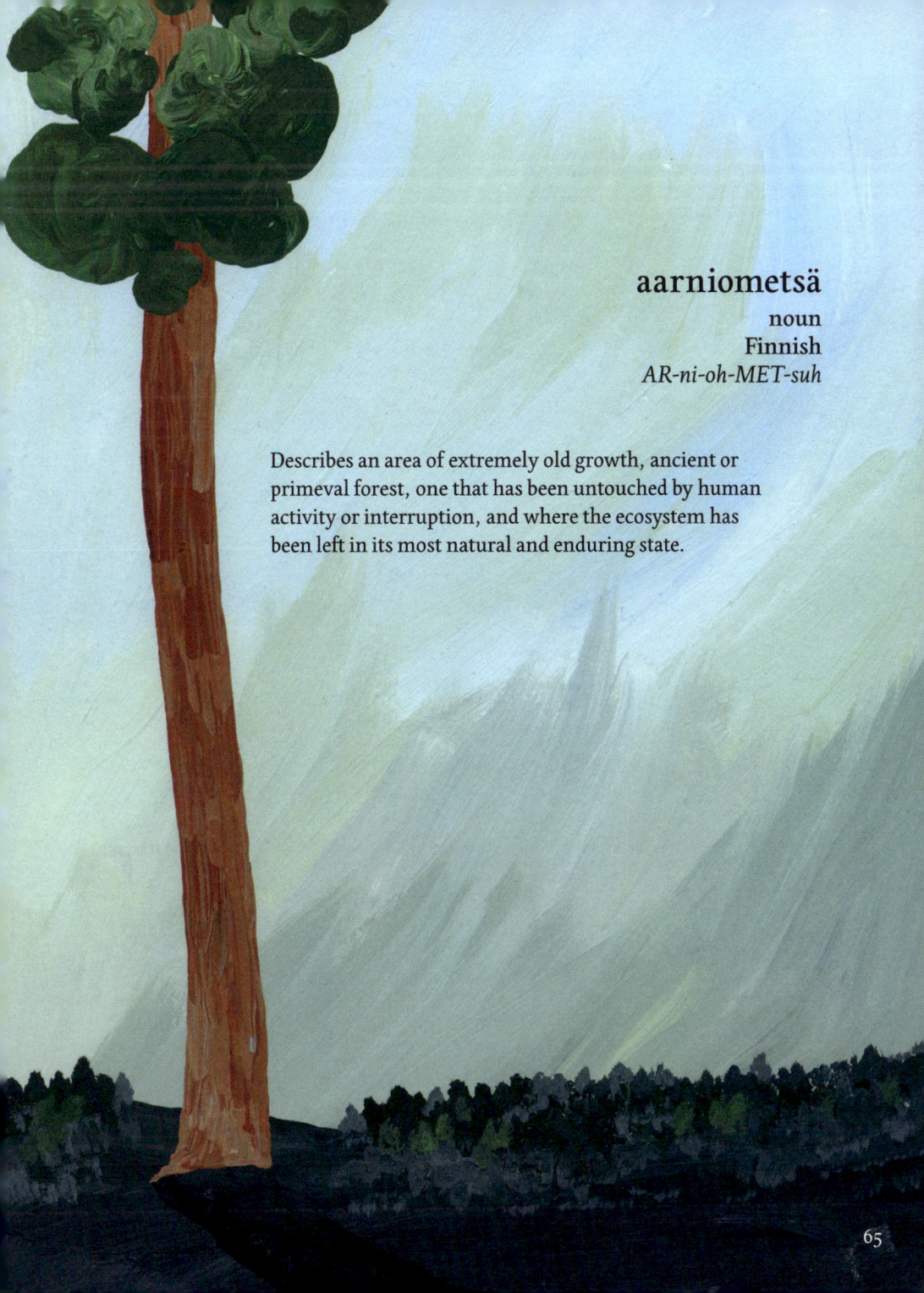

aarniometsä
noun
Finnish
AR-ni-oh-MET-suh

Describes an area of extremely old growth, ancient or primeval forest, one that has been untouched by human activity or interruption, and where the ecosystem has been left in its most natural and enduring state.

glas
adjective
Cornish
glaaz

Living, natural green, or the color of the sea, is *glas*, which also means blue and can mean other colors of the sea and plant life such as silver and grey. The word *gwyrdh*, meaning artificial green, entered the Cornish language (Kernewek) when the Roman empire crashed into Cornwall.

Glasneth refers to vegetation, or uncultivated land.

salicetum

noun
English
sal-ee-SEE-tum

Borrowed from the Latin *salictum*, *salicetum* is a word for a grove or thicket of willow trees.

Waldsterben
noun
German, New Coinage
VALT-shtur-ben

Literally means 'forest death' and refers to trees dying from things such as acid rain, or infection and disease, generally from human-induced atmospheric pollution, coined in the 1970s to initially reference the immense degree of tree decline in central Europe. In English, the equivalent term would be 'forest dieback.'

earthshine
noun
English
URTH-shine

The glow resulting from the sun's light, as reflected by Earth, and subsequently illuminating the darker portion of a crescent moon – the dark side of the moon managing to catch the Earth's leftovers.

ortzimuga

noun
Euskara
ORT-zi-mu-guh

From the words *ortzi* (sky) and *muga* (limit), a term for the horizon – the limit of the sky, what appears as the end of the land.

Time

Or: *The light changes a million times a day, which can save you*

The more time I manage to live through, the more I am convinced that the changing light across the passing of time can save a person. Save a person from madness, from despair, from numbness, from apathy, from excess.

By light, I mean the grey-blue embrace of dusk in winter and that it stays for only a handful of moments; and I mean the orange of earliest summer reflected in a black river; and I mean the light of Southern Europe that keeps painters painting; and I mean the filtered light through fresh thin leaves; I mean the midday light hitting the green gloss of a magpie's side; I mean the barely there light of the darkened Northern Hemisphere at the winter solstice and how you can rest or hide the tired parts of yourself within it; I mean the squares of sunlight that move from wall to wall throughout the course of a day; I mean the bleak weakness of February light that barely bothers to make an appearance this far north; and I mean the cloud-filtered light stretching itself across hillsides. Light saves us in its complexity and shape-shifting, in its ripening of food and memory, in its always, always returning no matter how dark the night.

Within a single language it is hard to have enough adequately descriptive words for the array of light we experience – an already narrow slice of a spectrum far larger than our human eyes will ever know. The slice of light we do observe has been explained and named, wavelengths numbered, acronyms suggested, a permanent rainbow to live by. Science and literature have threaded light differently, stitched very different tapestries from it, and as consciously lost as we are in those tapestries, we would do well to look up from them and just *look*. Time passes, light changes, we miss so much of it.

Time passing can be understood in terms of light, and it can also be understood in terms of the shape of a year, a season, a day, an hour, the blink of an eye, a lifetime. It is natural that we feel differently at different times of the day, exerting and resting, busying ourselves in daylight before returning to a burrow at the closing of night. Natural that we often find both time and light holding the instructions for feeling certain ways and for making certain choices – how the earliest blue morning hours are frequently the time when anxiety will rise like sap to the bodily surface, or how an equatorial midday sun will suggest retreating inside. In a few small planetary pockets, there remains more of a natural alignment with time, communities still living in cycles of light and temperature, but broadly speaking, a dismissal and disrespect of time has taken hold of us, and we struggle against its current, staying up at all hours on screens, resting for bare minimums, congratulating ourselves on some kind of conquering, some kind of override. Time goes on around us unaffected, unimpressed.

The light at certain times of day can help save you from any number of maladies, but it is necessary to know and accept it will also leave you behind, preferring as it does to remain eight minutes and twenty seconds ahead. We are illuminated by time and left behind by light. This apartness lends itself to wondering why almost all of your waking moments seem to be spent working, why it is cripplingly expensive to just exist and breathe as a person, why taking your time and loitering over anything is frowned upon. If living aligned with natural time, as opposed to against and despite it, had been viewed as an essential right of our now flailing and fatigued animal bodies, we would surely have never reached this point of complete planetary pain.

To live inside of time is to notice light. It requires releasing the already-crumbling grip on productivity and performance and to sometimes just stop: to observe and feel the movement of the sun's arc, to slow down enough that it is possible to feel how time is choosing to reside in the closest body – your own. For a person to begin to distinguish during the course of a day between the layers of lights and darks.

To live outside of time then is to feel impatient with the necessity of dark resting hours, to hurry time through unnaturally constrained shapes, to try and contort it into something that can have a bottom line, to say there is never enough of it, to try and hold it fiscally accountable. By living outside and unnoticing of time, we are misaligned with all of the small moments that could otherwise be memory and knowing. By trying to outpace time, we have left behind the earthly rhythms that were supposed to guide us, that were supposed to hold us close, and we urgently need to go back and retrieve them.

These rhythms are contained within light, within dark, within the 1 million things happening every moment of aliveness relative to temperature and time and everything we cannot see. It is most possible to notice or find the rhythms at the quieter times of day, when the mind has been allowed to retreat from tasks to simply observing, when away from fluorescent hallways, when remembering that you are one single person among billions and that you have the right to look absentmindedly at the briefest pink-orange light of early evening clouds whenever it feels like the thing to do.

úht-cearu

noun
Old English
OOHT-cheh-ah-roo

A word from Old English literally translated as 'early morning care' and referring to the kind of cares or worries that arrive to a person along with the early hours of a morning; the worries that gather as a person tosses and turns before dawn. *Úht*, meaning the time just before day breaks, and *cearu* (alternatively spelled *caru*), meaning worry, anxiety, sorrow or care.

Úht-cearu is an unease, the anxiety that can stretch out early morning, pre-dawn hours into a slow, blue lifetime.

(An *úht-floga* would be a creature that flies before dawn.)

madrugada

noun
Portuguese, Spanish
mah-droo-GAH-dah

Variously, the earliest hours of the morning before dawn, the period between midnight and sunrise, or sometimes simply dawn, in Portuguese another term for which is *alborada*.

The plural is *madrugadas*, and to awaken in the early hours of the morning is *madrugar* (pronounced *mah-droo-GAHR*).

gökotta
noun
Swedish
YUR-koh-tah

Meaning 'in the dawn hours,' *gökotta* first described the folk tradition of going bird-watching with the express purpose of hearing a *gök* (cuckoo) sing – the Old Swedish word *otta* meaning the time in between night and morning.

Gökotta has more recently moved to mean the practice of waking up early enough in the morning to appreciate the still and quietness of nature, to absorb its dawn benefits and, just maybe, though I doubt it is the sole purpose of many, to listen to birdsong.

In Swedish folklore, the cuckoo's call could predict different fates depending on the direction from which the bird's call was heard: *Södergök är dödergök, östergök är tröstegök. Nordegök är sorgegök, västergök är bästergök.*

(A cuckoo from the south is the death-cuckoo. A cuckoo from the east is the consolation-cuckoo. A cuckoo from the north is the sorrow-cuckoo. A cuckoo from the west is the best-cuckoo.)

霞 / xiá
noun
Mandarin
shee-ah

The way the clouds look at sunrise or sunset, a red-pink afterglow.

ṣubḥ kāḏib / صُبْح كَاذِب
noun
Arabic
SOO-bh KAH-thib

Meaning 'false dawn' and referring to the thin, weak light that arrives to eastern skies about an hour before the actual dawn – a zodiacal glow preceding sunrise. In English, 'false dawn' can be used figuratively to mean something hopeful amounting to not very much.

meriggiare
verb
Italian
meh-re-JAR-reh

Coming from the word *meriggio*, which means noon or midday, and mainly used in literature, *meriggiare* means to rest in the shade during the hottest hours of a day. It means the afternoon is passing, similar to how *albeggiare* describes the passing of dawn.

Outdated in everyday speech but used as a literary verb and known by many Italians from the title of a 1925 poem by Eugenio Montale, 'Meriggiare pallido e assorto' ('Noonday sleep, pale and lost in thought'), in which he describes a meriggiare in the countryside, seemingly amid a small existential crisis.

controra

noun
Italian
kon-TROH-rah

Typically found within southern Italian dialects, *controra* literally means 'against-hour' and refers to the time of day or around lunch hours, when it is far too hot to be outside, to do much at all aside from existing in the shade, or indoors – taking a siesta, or *pennichella*. Hot enough that the city streets quieten, and any person who braves going out at controra (*alla controra*) is viewed as a little foolish.

സൂര്യാസ്തമയം / sūryāstamayaṁ
noun
Malayalam
soo-YASTA-mai-um

The everyday sinking of the sun below the horizon; sunset.

Abendrot
noun
German
AH-bend-ROOHT

Literally translating as 'evening red,' *Abendrot* refers to the hues of a sky at sunset.

grimlins

noun
Orcadian Scots
GRIM-lins

With a dialect shaped by Scottish and Old Norse, and once a land of the Picts with their since lost languages, Orkney still holds some of its own special terms. *Grimlins* is one such word, derived from the Norwegian *grimla*, meaning to glimmer or twinkle, and defined by the *Dictionaries of the Scots Language* as 'twilight, the first or last gleams of daylight.'

Grimlins has also been written and recorded as *grimm(e)lings*, *grimplins*, *grimleens* and *grumlins*. Akin to gloaming, grimlins are the midsummer hours when it can be hard to tell if a day is beginning or ending.

Also of Orkney: *brae*, meaning a hill or mound; *gutter*, meaning mud; *holm*, meaning a small island; *loons*, meaning a marshland; and *skelp*, meaning a large extent of land.

sutemos
noun
Lithuanian
SUH-teh-mohs

Meaning after dark, dusk, twilight hours.

súton
noun
Croatian
soo-TOHN

Meaning twilight, though can also be used to refer to the end of something.

camhanaich

noun
Scottish Gaelic
kav-an-AECH

A word for half-light, twilight, though usually of the morning. *Camhanaich an latha* in Scottish Gaelic (Gàidhlig) would translate as morning twilight, and *camhanaich na h-oidhche* refers to evening twilight.

In a handful of languages, dusk:

crepúsculo (Portuguese, *creh-POOS-coo-loh*)

cyfnos (Welsh, *KUHV-nos*)

shom (Uzbek, *shom*, written as *Шом* in Tajik but pronounced the same)

magharibi (Swahili, *mah-gah-REE-bee*)

amurg (Romanian, *ah-MOORG*)

бүрэнхий / *bürenkhii* (Mongolian, *bohr-en-HHI*)

شفق / *shafaq* (Farsi, *SHA-faq*)

황혼 / *hwanghon* (Korean, *hwang-hon*)

गोधूलि / *godhūli* (Hindi, *GOHD-hoo-lee*,
written গোধূলি in Bengali but pronounced the same)

மாலை / *maalai* (Tamil, *MAH-ah-lay*)

krēsla (Latvian, *KRAS-luh*)

amhdhorchacht (Irish, *awv-GHURRA-khukht*, translated as 'gloaming,' literally 'uncooked darkness')

ilunabarra (Euskara, *ee-LOO-na-bah-rah*)

الغَسَق / *al-Ghasaq* (Arabic, *al-GHA-saq*)

сутінки / *sutinky* (Ukrainian, *soo-TIEN-keh*)

fiidkii (Somali, *fee-ID-kee*)

ზეგ / zeg
noun
Georgian
zeg

Meaning the day after tomorrow, while მაზეგ (*mazeg*) refers to the day after the day after tomorrow. While on the subject of time:

The archaic English *overmorrow*, to mean the day after tomorrow, and the German *Übermorgen*, to mean the same. In Spanish the word *anteayer*, to mean the day before yesterday; the archaic English *ereyesterday*, to mean the same. In Hindi परसों (*parsõ*), to mean both the day before yesterday *and* the day after tomorrow, and कल (*kal*), meaning both yesterday and tomorrow. The English *antejentacular*, meaning before breakfast.

And in Icelandic, the delight that is referring to a nonspecific or not-remembered date or time in the past using *sautján hundruð og súrkál*, or 'seventeen hundred and sauerkraut.'

月見 / tsukimi

noun
Japanese
tsu-kee-mee

Literally meaning 'moon-viewing' or 'looking at the moon,' *tsukimi* or *otsukimi* (お月見) is the Japanese practice, tradition – dating back more than 1,000 years to the Heian period, with aristocrats holding parties on boats, or in pavilions and gardens, offering poetry or seasonal produce while beholding the moon – and present-day festival of viewing and celebrating the full autumnal moon. Tsukimi itself was influenced heavily by Chinese cultural traditions, ones still practised today, called 中秋節 (*zhōngqiūjié*).

If the day arrives and the full moon is obscured by clouds or other weather, celebrations will still go ahead, but there are specific terms for if there is no moon (無月, *mugetsu*) or a rainy moon (雨月, *ugetsu*).

plenilune
adjective
English
PLEN-uh-loon

Pertaining to the full moon: either characteristic of a full moon, or resembling one. From the Latin for full moon, *plēnilūnium*. In contrast, *novilunar* would be of, or pertaining to, a new moon.

చందమామ / chandamama
noun
Telugu
CHAN-duh-mah-mah

Translating literally as 'moon uncle,' the term refers affectionately to the moon in its most comforting, endearing guise.

tunglmyrkvi
noun
Icelandic
TOONGL-mir-kvi

Refers to a lunar eclipse but literally means 'moon-darkness,' with *myrkvi* coming from *myrkur*, meaning darkness.

trasnochar

verb
Spanish
trahs-noh-CHAHR

An excess of night. *Trasnochar* is to stay up particularly late, or even all night. The usage varies between Spanish-speaking countries, but in Argentina, a *trasnochado* can not only be someone who has stayed up all night long but also someone who simply looks completely exhausted. When used as an adjective as opposed to a verb, trasnochar means 'outdated.'

Related is *desvelarse* (pronounced *dehs-beh-LAHR-seh*), describing waking up in the middle of the night: having been unable to adequately sleep in the first instance, waking, then being unable to fall back asleep.

luscofusco

noun
Galician
LOOS-koh-foos-koh

Luscofusco refers to nightfall, the final rays of sun. Likely from the Latin *lusco*, meaning 'one-eyed'; or *reluscar*, 'to flash'; and *fusco*, meaning 'dark.' Exists in the Portuguese language, too.

Another beautiful sun-related Galician (Galego) term is *raxeira* (pronounced *RRHA-shei-rah*), which refers to the lines or patterns drawn by window-filtered sunlight on surfaces.

ótta

noun
Icelandic
OH-tta

An old Icelandic system of keeping time, called *Eykt*, which divides the solar day into eight pieces known as *eyktarmörk* – *ótta* was the word for 3 a.m. but also a word for fear, with *óttalaus* meaning to be without fear.

The other times of day were:

miðnætti (midnight)

rismál (6 a.m.)

dagmál (9 a.m.)

hádegi (noon)

nón (3 p.m.)

miðaftann (6 p.m.)

náttmál (9 p.m.)

skúmaskot

noun
Icelandic
SKOO-mah-skot

Translating as dark, ominous corners or nooks, *skúmaskot* encapsulates the feeling of and preference for spending time in the more shadowy places, referring also to the dark corners themselves – it is, for example, possible to lose one's keys in a skúmaskot.

tharurru

noun
Ngarluma
tah-ROOR-ruh

Estimated to have fewer than twenty fluent speakers left, Ngarluma is the language of the Indigenous Ngarluma people of coastal northwestern Australia. The word *tharurru* describes all at once: dusk, the glow of evening, a peace of mind.

Water

Or: *Glass half full, glass half empty,
but have you tried swimming*

It would have been remiss not to provide water with its own chapter. Without it, we would be as paper and dust and salt, crystalline beings without so much as a single breath to share between billions. Without water, there is no life as we know and need and love it. A planet without oceans, without rain, without green. Instinctively, we know its deep importance, and this instinct, much like those instincts of season and time, has been buried under a sludge of greed and taken-for-granted-ness. Water has gone from revered to monetized, from protected and sacred to globally polluted. Sometimes it seems humans cannot be trusted to take care of the most beautiful and most basic things.

We are supposed to revere water, trust it, respect the way in which it keeps everything alive, respiring. Every single person on this Earth could have had clean, safe water to drink, and rivers could have remained in their slowed, ever-changing serpentine bends, but instead, we have flooded the seas with plastic, demanded rivers be straight, and decided that human thirst was not created equal. Rain falls on soils empty of nutrients, chemicals are washed out of concrete pipes into waterways, whales swallow plastic as part of their ever-diminishing aquatic meals. Some are made sick drinking their tap water, some scarcely have access to water at all, and in other cases, it finds itself branded and bottled and sold on shelves by multinational corporations.

Some shapes of water I do not recognize: the anaerobic swamps on roadsides, the puddle iridescent with engine oil, the miles-wide sprinkler systems watering thousands of acres of malnourished farmland. Some shapes of water I can recognize: the left-alone river as it curves itself gently over and through land, the first rain that smells of summer, the fall of a single drop from the point of a leaf, the crash felt in the body when standing close enough to the ocean's edge, a wild thing lowering its head to drink, snowmelt, the dizzying reflection of sky in a perfectly still surface, the shrouding of hillsides in mist, the way small depressions in rock can hold on to the liquid for longer than seems reasonable.

Water can choose to run throughout and across anything, and within it, we can choose to be made weightless, ethereal, oceanic. As animals without scales or fur, we are able to move through water in ways that can feel at once therapeutic, ritualistic and ancient. Our oldest myths are often watery ones, its power inscribed within a great many cultures, and I believe it is not too late to write more. I have been some of the happiest iterations of myself within water, either swimming out into the merciful repetition of waves or across a flat southern sea to a small wooden pontoon, or feet tucked into a river's edge while lying back onto millennia-smoothed yet still uncomfortable stones. A body within an eddy, a body through a wave, a body remembering what it feels like to exist in an environment apart from any culturally induced tension. The act of swimming is not for everybody, is not safe for everybody, but it cannot help but return you to a time when you existed as atoms, as animal.

Water seems to me unapologetic, a lesson in providing and retrieving, and a path to follow back to the source – there are still fish who can remember in places where we have forgotten. Our choice of care or carelessness for the bodies of others seems inextricably linked to that choice of care or carelessness toward not only water but all aspects of nature, and it would be understandable to look around and conclude that an active carelessness has become the standard way of being for most people. I think, though, that people *want* to care, that it actively – albeit sometimes subconsciously – hurts them not to, and that there is an indescribable force that accompanies demonstrating overt care for both people and place.

There are days when I walk the long way around back home from somewhere or other, a route that usually takes me across a sad, bright green stretch of manicured golf course to the river path, a small creek running between road and river and slicing the golf course in half. On two separate occasions now, I have seen an older man in waders moving slowly down the creek and toward the river, when the water level is low and gentle, attentively picking out fragments of trash before they have an opportunity to join the larger watercourse. Both times, I have waved and smiled, said something inconsequential or even idiotically enthused, but the fact that *he is there*, removing perhaps ten or twenty pieces of plastic each time, is to me a confirmation that most 'ordinary' people want to care, to help, to try in any way they can to heal the planet. To help even if they receive nothing in return, to help even if their actions aren't funded and externally validated. And yes, there are others who, often through no fault of their own, are scarred by apathy and neglect, but that number is the smaller one, and the care is always louder if you're looking for it.

Once, while walking over a small bridge crossing that same creek, I noticed a saturated cuboid cardboard object down in the water and clambered down to retrieve what turned out to be used-up fireworks – surprisingly heavy – as I didn't much like the thought of it sitting in there, getting washed to who knows where. We are built from, and remembered by, our choices.

The words that follow are guides down to the water's edge, to the personalities of rain, to the wide and unfathomable reaches of an ocean, to storms and glimmering reflections, and to sometimes taking shelter but sometimes standing out in the wet. Saturation as salvation, swimming as a safe passage through the mire of modernity. There are words guiding us to the odours of estuaries, to entering into cold water, as reminders that our use of the word *body* to describe both ourselves and stretches of water is perhaps not something to be overlooked but rather something to be read into.

渚 / nagisa

noun
Japanese
nah-gee-sah

Used to convey a quiet, reflective relationship with water's edge, and evoking both the image and feeling of a calm shoreline – used less in everyday language and more in poetic contexts, or place-names. The literal patterns made by waves would be 波紋 (*hamon*) or, for the associated ripples, 漣 (*sazanami*).

curglaff

noun
Scots
KUR-glaff

Formed from *cur*, a prefix that intensifies in meaning, and *glaff*, as a variation of *gliff*, meaning a glimpse or glint, together then referring to a sharp but brief sensation, such as the bracing shock of entering very cold water. Considered archaic and dialectical, it is noted in John Jamieson's *An Etymological Dictionary of the Scottish Language* of 1808.

amipushu

noun
Innu-aimun
ahm-poh-HOH

Describes water that is quiet and calm on its surface.

In Innu-aimun, as with various other First Nations languages, it is possible to compose words with such complex, nuanced meanings that it would need a whole sentence or more to be translated, into English or otherwise – known as a polysynthetic language. Words within Innu-aimun can contain remarkable detail about landscapes, creatures and plants – for instance, there are around twenty different words for caribou, each of which holds detail about the age or physical appearance of the caribou in question.

An example of a single watery word containing such detail might be *nutinakamishtin* (the breeze has made small ripples on the lake, pronounced *nuat-NAH-kamish-IN*).

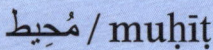 / muḥīṭ
noun
Arabic
mu-HEET

Meaning ocean, literally translating as 'whole,' or surrounding completely, a circumference.

There are many words for sea, or ocean, in Arabic, others being قاموس (qāmūs, pronounced ka-mus), an obsolete word for ocean, which also means 'dictionary' and comes from a root meaning to immerse, and بَحْر (baḥr, pronounced ba-h'r), which means 'sea,' but also refers to poetic metre, the rhythmic structure.

madwebiisaa
inanimate intransitive verb
Ojibwemowin
mah-dway-bee-SA

Meaning you can hear the rain, or that the rain can be heard, literally 'be heard raining.'

Ojibwe refers to a particular Anishinaabe nation of people, and Ojibwemowin and Anishinaabemowin are both used to refer to the language spoken by the Ojibwe, itself with many dialects, though Anishinaabemowin is a more general term for an Indigenous language – *mo* means language, or speaks, and *win* turns the word into a noun.

It is a language of verbs – 80 percent verbs compared to English with its 30 percent – and in a beautiful, rare way, doesn't borrow vocabulary from the outside, rather it constantly renews and expands itself from the land, an example of this being the term for carbon dioxide, *mitigoo-inanaamowin*, which translates literally to 'the air that trees breathe.' Within Ojibwemowin, everything has agency, both the animate and the inanimate, and so verbs are constantly altered and added to (an agglutinative language) in order to better describe things.

petrichor
noun
English, New Coinage
PE-tri-kor

First coined by Australian mineral scientists Isabel Joy Bear and Richard Grenfell Thomas, within a paper published in the journal *Nature* in 1964, who originally proposed the word to replace what was previously called 'argillaceous odor,' or the scent following rainfall on dry ground – this scent coming from the release of plant oils, volatile compounds secreted by microorganisms, geosmin and ozone.

Petrichor has now expanded to mean not only rainfall following a dry phase but also the smell *before* rainfall, and has migrated into 'petrichor effect,' which describes the emotional response that can be triggered by the scent.

The word itself is formed from the Greek πέτρα *(petra)*, meaning rock or stone, and ἰχώρ *(ichōr)*, which refers in Greek mythology to the liquid that flowed in the veins of the Gods in place of blood.

potamichor

noun
English, New Coinage
po-TAM-ee-kor

Coined by the Welsh philosopher Ginny Battson to name the particular odour of rivers. Made from the Greek ποτάμι (*potámi*), meaning river, and ἰχώρ (*ichōr*) as with petrichor. Battson has also proposed *ekvolichor* for estuary and salt marsh odours, *limnichor* for the smell of lakes, *limnoulichor* for the smell of a pond, and *telmichor* for the scent of bog.

மண்வாசனை / manvasanai

noun
Tamil
mann-VAH-sah-nay

Literally 'earth,' or 'soil scent,' with மண் (*man*) meaning soil and வாசனை (*vasanai*) meaning smell or aroma, and in this way, a blood relative of petrichor. In the Tamil language, vowels, of which there are twelve, are categorized based on the duration of sound, and the word மாத்திரை (*maathirai*) is used as a unit of time for these sounds, equivalent to the time needed to blink once. These twelve letters can be subdivided into two main categories, குறில் (*kuril*) and நெடில் (*nedil*), with kuril being shorter in sound, one maathirai in length, and nedil longer, lasting two maathirai. Some consonants can even be half a maathirai in length, which I've tried to measure with my own eyelids and which seemed confusingly difficult to my slow, cold, Northern Hemisphere eyes.

chrysalism

noun
English, New Coinage
KRIS-uh-liz-uhm

Freshly defined in 2015 by the writer John Koenig to mean the feeling and quality of being inside during a storm. The word *chrysalism* also has archaic use in the early 1800s to mean either a state of transition, or a state of dormancy and rest.

Likely from the Latin *chrysalis*, meaning pupa of a butterfly or moth.

aranyhíd

noun
Hungarian
AH-ran-yi-hid

Literally meaning 'golden bridge,' *aranyhíd* is a word for the glistening, golden reflection of the sun either rising or setting on the surface of water. For the moon, the equivalent is *ezüsthíd*, or 'silver bridge' (pronounced *EZ-oohst-id*).

yakamoz
noun
Turkish
YAH-kah-moz

Another word for the reflection of moonlight, though in this case also used to describe any sort of lights shimmering on water, translating as something far more inadequate, like 'sparkling sea.' Originally its definition lay in an ocean biology context to mean the phosphorescence in the sea caused by bioluminescent tiny things.

In Turkish, the word *mehtap* means moonlight, and *gumusservi* (pronounced *gu-muh-SAIR-vee*) also seems to be used to refer to moonlight on water, though literally it refers to a silver cypress.

mareel

noun
Shetland
muh-REEL

Translated as 'sea-fire,' *mareel* is the luminous, sparkling phosphorescence observed in the ocean, especially on autumn nights, and that can also be seen on fish in the darkness.

Shetland, Shaetlan to native speakers, has been historically repressed and stigmatized, though it is increasingly studied in academic contexts, and there are ongoing concerted efforts to distinguish it from Scots. A living and everyday tongue spoken by 30 to 50 percent of the approximately 23,000 residents, the language has a large Norse influence – a now-extinct dialect of Norse, Norn, was still present in the islands up until the mid-nineteenth century and is responsible for much of the grammar, with the Scots ancestor providing much of the vocabulary. Speakers of Scandinavian languages would sense something familiar yet unusual about Shetland, something you cannot quite put a finger on; such is the relationship between these languages, and it's important to note that Shetland is not mutually intelligible with any other Scots variants aside from those in Orkney and Caithness, which are formerly Norn-speaking places.

The words of the islands are themselves knitted into a deep and felt connection to the water and the land. They include *stripe*, describing a small rivulet or creek; *daalamist*, referring to a mist gathered by a valley overnight that dissipates with sunrise; *grummel*, to make water muddy by stirring up sediment; *moder dy*, describing a specific kind of underlying sea swell and used by experienced *haaf men*, or fishermen, as a guide; *speet*, a heavy rain shower. It is worth noting, too, that Shetland words have a fascinating and bewildering variety of spellings within differing dialectal and sociolectal writings.

kłúsx̌nítkʷ

noun
Nsqilxʷcen
OOS-kha-nidt

Nsqilxʷcen is the language of the Sqilxʷ Okanagan people, who are Indigenous to British Columbia in Canada and Washington State in the United States. The word *kłúsx̌nítkʷ* describes either a body of water or a place that has two long sides.

川明かり / kawaakari

noun
Japanese
kah-wah-a-kah-ree

Kawaakari is the gleam of a river in the dark, in the dusk, a compound word formed from the term for river, 川 (*kawa*), and the term for light or illumination, 明かり (*akari*). Found in literature and classical aesthetics, in seasonal haiku and in descriptions of soft, quiet evening scenes, kawaakari can refer to moonlight, or lanterns, or even the glow from our electricity-wired cities.

offing
noun
English
OHFF-ing

Meaning the part of an ocean that is visible from the shore, the deeper sea. Also found in the phrase 'in the offing' to mean in the near, or foreseeable, future, or something within sight but distanced.

lacuna
noun
English
luh-KOO-nuh

A gap, break or missing piece, usually within a text or musical work, within paintings, or within an argument. In a botanical context, it refers to the air gaps inside the cellular tissue of plants. Comes from the Latin for lake, *lacus*, with *lacūna* in Latin meaning less figurative gaps and more a literal hole, like a pond or a small pool.

I propose the idea of returning *lacuna* more intentionally to its meaning of small pool, as in the collections of water that happen throughout landscapes and that one might, say, stumble across while out walking – a lacuna within a rock formation, a lacuna as a tide pool, a lacuna leftover after flooding has subsided.

tweavelet

noun
English, New Coinage
TWEEV-let

Also coined by Ginny Battson, *tweavelet* gives a name to the leaves and small twigs caught and held in place by other branches or trees following a flood or other high waters.

ammil
noun
English, Devonian
AAM-il

Believed to be derived from the Early Modern English *ammel*, which literally means 'enamel,' *ammil* is a word fallen out of general usage but still found within the countryside and among farmers of Devon referring to the ice that can coat every fence post, every fern frond, every leaf, every twig-end, every rock, so formed when a sunny winter thawing has been interrupted by a large drop in temperature, resulting in a sight quite astonishing to the eyes on a cold, sunlit morning.

சாரல் / cāral

noun
Tamil
SSA-rul

Drizzling, thin rain, such as the sort of rain arriving secondarily from a waterfall, or from clouds perched on mountains.

serein

adjective
French
SURR-un

Referring specifically to a fine rain that falls from cloudless skies after the sun has set, or during early morning hours. In Middle French, the word had the meaning of evening or nightfall. In English, *serene* has the same meaning as serein in its noun form, the plural being *serenes*.

gully washer
noun
English, American
GUH-lee WAH-sher

A short, extremely heavy downpour of rain, a sudden deluge – which can also be referred to as a *cloudburst*. *Gully washer* is chiefly found in the Midwestern and Western United States.

hyetal
adjective
English
HY-eh-tuhl

Meaning of or belonging to rain, pertaining to rain, or simply rainy regions of a place, rainfall generally. Comes from the Greek ὑετός (*huetós*, meaning rain).

nāulu

noun
Hawaiian
NAH-oo-lu

Rain in Hawaiian is *ua*, and *nāulu* describes a sudden rain shower, one that passes quickly, perhaps a reason why the word can also refer to the state of feeling angry or vexed – usually also something that is best to pass through quickly. Nāulu is also the name of a specific sea breeze at Kawaihae. There are countless names and stories enveloping rain in Hawaiʻi), here are just a few more:

koko, either when a rain brings a rainbow or is heavy enough to muddy streams red-brown; this rain is also called *ua koko*, which means 'blood-red rain'

kuāua, a soft rain that tells a farmer it is time to plant sweet potatoes

Poʻonui, a heavy, troublesome rain, literally meaning 'big head,' the kind of rain that chills the spine

Waʻahila, a soft, sweeping rain found at Waʻahila between two valleys

заструга / zastruga

noun
Russian
zah-STROO-gah

Also written as *sastruga*, *zastruga* refers to the eroded wave-like snow ridges formed by the wind in polar landscapes. The plural is *zastrugi* or *sastrugi*.

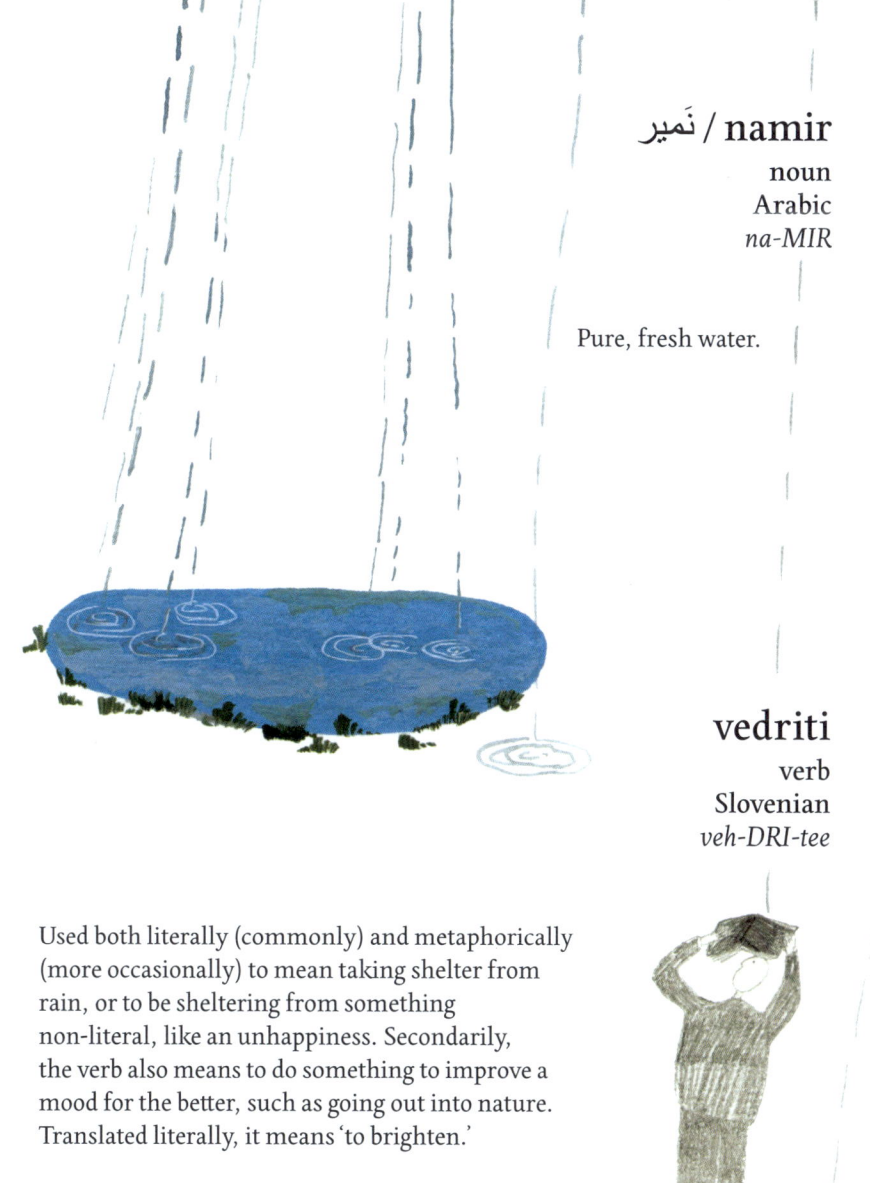

نَمير / **namir**
noun
Arabic
na-MIR

Pure, fresh water.

vedriti
verb
Slovenian
veh-DRI-tee

Used both literally (commonly) and metaphorically (more occasionally) to mean taking shelter from rain, or to be sheltering from something non-literal, like an unhappiness. Secondarily, the verb also means to do something to improve a mood for the better, such as going out into nature. Translated literally, it means 'to brighten.'

雷声大,雨点小 / léishēng dà, yǔdiǎn xiǎo
idiom
Cantonese
loi-sing-dai, yu-dim-siu

Translates as 'loud thunder, but tiny raindrops' and is used to infer that much is being talked about or proclaimed but very little action is actually being taken.

Using the method of romanization called Jyutping (developed by the Linguistic Society of Hong Kong in 1993), the phonetic Cantonese pronunciations use six numbers at the end of syllables to indicate tone contours, and would have the phrase above like so: leoi[4] sing[1] daai[6] jyu[5] dim[2] siu[2].

Tone 1 is 'high level,' tone 2 'high rising,' tone 3 'mid level,' tone 4 'low falling,' tone 5 'low rising,' and tone 6 'low level.'

utu

noun
Finnish
OO-toh

The word *utu* technically refers to a light, usually morning mist sitting close to the ground and is translated as mist or haze. *Usva* (pronounced *OOS-vah*), meanwhile, refers to a near-ground mist that is thicker than utu and is translated as haze or fog, and *sumu* (pronounced *SOO-moh*) is used when the water vapour obscures visibility, more of a fog.

The three seem too often be used interchangeably, though if a mist is caused by something other than water vapour, the word *auer* (pronounced *OW-aire*) is used instead.

erämaajärvi

noun
Finnish
EH-RAH-mah-yehr-vi

> While it has meant other things at times, *erämaa* refers in current usage to remote areas of forest and wilderness that support the ecosystems as they are and as they should be – old-growth trees, undrained bogs, undammed watercourses. *Erämaajärvi* refers to a lake in such an area of wilderness, and is also found in *erämaa-alueet*, which are wilderness areas established in the northernmost Lapland region of Finland in part to protect Indigenous Sámi culture.

linnunmaito

noun
Finnish
LIN-oon-mai-toh

Translated as nectar but literally meaning 'bird-milk,' it can be used to describe water that is a perfect, comfortable temperature to swim in.

soodraght

noun
Manx
SOO-drakht

Sounding very much like the thing it describes, *soodraght* is the sound of waves crashing onto a shore, backwash, the rolling of the ocean, said by some to only be audible on the Isle of Man (in Manx the name of the island is *Ellan Vannin*). The endonym (the native English word for a people, place or language) for Manx is Gaelg, or Gailck – the word specifically for the name of a language within that language itself is *autoglottonym*.

Weather

Or: *It's all we ever talk about,*
and am I the only one who dreams of monsoons

I've always found the idea of accurately trying to predict incoming weather using technology slightly strange, somehow off-kilter. Useful and practical, I'm sure, but something about the standing of a lone, smartly suited person in front of a blindingly bright digital screen gesturing to this or that sits uncomfortably for me, sits impersonal. Our preference to harness and thereby control weather is only one of many impositions inflicted on natural systems, but as with other things, it marks and consistently ingrains a kind of separation between patterns of weather and our daily choices. We want to carry on with plans regardless of rainfall, regardless of extreme winds, regardless of a large snowfall. To many, weather is an inconvenience to be overcome rather than an ever-changing astonishment to be experienced.

For something that reaches into and impacts every single crevice of the planet, we use relatively few words day-to-day to describe it. It rains, or it doesn't. It might be noted as raining either heavily or lightly, but that is about it, and wind is generally only commented on when there is either an eerily complete lack of it or it's causing trees to fall groundward with nests being ripped from their branches. It is cold, or very cold, or unseasonably warm. The sun is unobstructed by clouds or it isn't, and there will always be someone to declare there is either too much or too little of it.

Have you ever noticed though how seabirds flying in high winds can look like small torn-up pieces of paper, as if tossed from a window, or how crepuscular rays appear to point toward earthly things, or how animals turn their stoic faces toward the warm sun, or how owls don't like to fly in rain, that everything is made greener by it, or how the heads of flowers will follow the sunlight, or how a covering of ice can cause you to second-guess yourself, or how it could take only a single day of strong wind for a cherry to lose every last blossom, or how much kinder people tend to be when they are warm?

At some point, we stopped shaping our days and needs in a close association with weather, stopped being able to sense it. As animals like any other we could certainly know it more deeply, wordlessly even, but this knowledge cannot be stumbled upon or prescribed, and there are so few communities left who live knowing their senses fully in this way. Weather used to be one of the most consistent patterns of this planet, and therefore a daily opportunity to notice the changing sensations of one's physical body. Our fluctuating temperatures, our comfort, the securing of a place in which to shelter or the lack of one, the tendency to seek out warmth.

The harshness or relentlessness of weather can turn friends to lovers, can cause others to lose their minds, can provoke travel across continents, can cancel plans, can reroute rivers, can flood civilizations, can incite both panic and delight, can wash away a life's work, can set fire to forests. It provides us with both fear and fascination, with an excuse, with something to say to those we only ever encounter as strangers. We want to be out in it, but we also want to know what it wants from us. Out in a rainstorm because sometimes that can be just as appealing as watching it from behind warm windows – there is a natural craving for weather to confirm one's aliveness, and as with storms the same can be true of being out in strong winds, or heavy snowfall, or dense mist. We want to feel alternately held by weather, lost in it, safe from it, overwhelmed by it, in cahoots with it, favoured by it, protected from it.

I dream of monsoons because I've never experienced them, because I'm certain that such a thing would mark some irreversible change in me, and because I want to know the word for 'monsoon' in twenty different saturated tongues.

And the always shadows, the shadows always. Made long by the weak winter light, made by the moon at its very brightest, made brief by birds flying across the sun, forever made by that sun even though it is 93 million miles away. Wind that moves the shadows of clouds slowly or swiftly across mountain ranges, shadows that ask nothing of you except to notice. Shadows that seem crisp at their edges and some that seem as though they are bleeding blurred into the ground. All more evidence of aliveness and the ever-changing nature of every last atom.

We talk about the weather because in doing so we are talking about being alive, and fleeting, and flawed. We talk about weather because we want people to know that we, too, can be changeable and varied and nourishing. The following words provide more ways to notice both oneself and the weather that constantly surrounds, makes light and dark of us. We need more words for weather because through the planetary destruction wrought we've altered its most essential and ancient patterns, perhaps in ways that now cannot be reversed or fully mended, and being able to recognize and name that which is abnormal seems an important minimum of going forward toward something. Rain will come, clouds will part, the sun will burn, and we will dream not only of monsoons but of a better and more beautiful world in order that we may one day live in it.

heavengravel

noun
English, Poetic
HEA-vun-gra-vuhl

In the poem 'The Loss of the Eurydice,' Gerard Manley Hopkins refers to hailstones as *heavengravel*. The poem commemorates a ship that sank during a freak snowstorm in 1878 that was reported by *The Midland Naturalist* as a 'violent but brief atmospheric disturbance':

'Heavengravel? wolfsnow, worlds of it, wind there?'

graupel

noun
English
GRAU-puhl

A meteorological term that has been in use since at least an 1889 weather report, *graupel* refers to a very specific kind of soft hail, which forms when supercooled water droplets adhere to falling snowflakes. Distinguishable from true hail, which is pure ice formed by thunderstorms. Graupel has also been called 'corn snow' and 'hominy snow,' and is Germanic in origin as a diminutive of *graupe*, which refers to a grain of pearl barley.

Supercooled water droplets freezing generally onto a surface – such as tree branches – are referred to as 'rime ice,' which is categorized as soft rime, hard rime or pure ice, all formed slightly differently.

Frischluftfanatiker
noun
German
FRISHT-lohft-fan-NAH-ti-ker

Meaning a person who is adamant about always having some degree of fresh air inside a house, no matter how cold that air is, or someone who is hell-bent on always being outside in it.

oogly
adjective
Cornish
OOG-lee

A word for how the sky looks when wild, dark, powerful weather is incoming.

resolana

noun
Spanish
rreh-soh-LAH-nah

Referring to a sun-specific kind of heat and light, or glare from the sun as reflected by surfaces, the kind that can be strong and hot enough to burn. Used most commonly in the context of a warning – be wary of *resolana*, because it can be present even if the sun is not visibly shining.

In the Mallorquín language, the equivalent would be *ressol* (pronounced *RRE-sol*).

zirimiri

noun
Euskara
SI-ri-MI-ri

In the Euskara language (called Basque in French and Vasco in Spanish) – the oldest living language in Europe with about 1 million speakers – *zirimiri* refers to a gentle, soft rain that can fall for hours, even days. An equivalent has been adopted into Spanish, in which it is written *sirimiri*.

Euskara is believed to be the only survivor of a European language family, prehistoric, referred to by most linguists as a 'language isolate,' and having no known connections to any other language. In a way, it is the only Indigenous European language, as it was present when the Indo-European languages, which now dominate the continent, arrived, infiltrated and were imposed – by the time of the Roman period much of Europe spoke Indo-European languages. Euskara is spoken in five dialects within the territories sitting either side of the Pyrenees mountain range, places in which the oldest Paleolithic sites and cave art also reside.

turadh

noun
Scottish Gaelic
TUR-ruhg

Meaning a subsiding of cloud, a pause between rain showers, or a period of dry weather.

Gaelic (Gàidhlig), as a language once shared by both Ireland and Western Scotland, has been spoken since at least 500 AD, and was the dominant language of the emerging kingdom of Scotland between 800 and 1100 AD, with its influence also found in the eastern part of the country, or the Lowlands. Other influences, primarily French and Dutch, followed as the Scottish monarchy widened its cultural and linguistic horizons, and subsequently, use of Gaelic declined, becoming identified almost solely with the west (the Highlands) and was actively persecuted and suppressed from the mid-eighteenth century onward during the Highland Clearances.

The term 'Scottish Gaelic' appeared around 1600, and the languages of Irish and Scottish Gaelic are distinct from each other, with mutual intelligibility between speakers not guaranteed and with each language having letter combinations not possible in the other. (One way to know which language you're looking at: In Scottish Gaelic the accents on letters always slant to the left, and in Irish, accents always slant to the right.)

gluggaveður
noun
Icelandic
GLUGG-ah-ve-thur

Literally translates as 'window weather' and refers to the sorts of weather that are pleasant to look at from inside but, depending on how one feels about such weathers, perhaps less pleasant to actually be outside in. A not uncommon phenomenon to be found in Iceland, a place of some unpredictable and harsh weathers, and the language features a long list of different words – possibly as many as 180 if including dialectical variations and compound words – to describe various types of wind and its characteristics, or wind-related weather. A few of these:

kaldi, cold wind

stinningskaldi, ice-cold wind

andvari, a breath of wind

kul, a light breeze

sunnablær, southern breeze

hvass or *hvassviðri*, gale

allhvass, moderate gale, a little more than hvass or hvassviðri

fárviðri, tempest

fellibylur, hurricane

gola, breeze

hnjúkapeyr, warm and dry mountain wind

sviptivindar, sudden strong wind

sandfok, the sand found within the wind

skafrenningur, conditions where wind has blown snow into fresh drifts

dúnalogn, completely still air, windless

Frühjahrsmüdigkeit

noun
German
FROO-yars-moo-dich-kite

Different from spring fever, or cabin fever, *Frühjahrsmüdigkeit* translates to 'spring fatigue' or 'spring lethargy' and refers to a tiredness brought on by the changing, and changeable, weather of spring; a changeable energy or mood to accompany the fluctuations in temperature and light.

sólarfrí

noun
Icelandic
SO-lar-free

Sólarfrí is a 'sun holiday,' meaning a day when employees are given – or simply take – unexpected time off from work with the express purpose of enjoying warm, sunny weather.

pogodnie

adjective
Polish
poh-GOHD-in-yeh

When used in the context of weather, *pogodnie* means brightly, or sunnily, weather that is simply pleasant. Can also be used to describe an attitude or disposition of a person.

brontide
noun
English
BRON-tide

Referring to a low, distant rumbling, sounding something like thunder, but thought to be caused by minor seismic shifts, earth tremors. Most likely to be heard along coastlines and near lakes, a sort of geological thunder.

dreich
adjective
Scots
driecch

Reportedly first recorded in 1420 to mean tedious or enduring, *dreich* means anything from grey, gloomy, damp weather, to protracted or wearisome, to something that extends for a long time or distance, even just dull or unenjoyable – can be used in the context of people, of weather, of time, of tasks, of journeys, of much anything at all. Used primarily today to mean either gloomy weather, or something tedious. Conversely, *braw* means fine, or pleasant.

Gaelic and Scots are entirely different and distinct languages, the true tongues of the country. Scots, along with English, is a surviving descendant of Anglo-Saxon dialects spoken in Scotland since 600 AD, and similarly to the divergence of Irish and Scottish Gaelic, Scots and English also gradually moved away from each other, with Scots absorbing Scandinavian, Dutch and French influences, among others. It was the dominant language of the Kingdom of Scotland, existing alongside Gaelic, before declining significantly after the forming of the United Kingdom of Great Britain in 1707, which saw English being moved to the position of official state language and the country's native languages subjected to great hostility and repression. After the Scottish parliament was formed in 1999, initiatives were introduced to encourage and rejuvenate both languages, and they are recognized officially as minority languages of the UK – Scots (also referred to as Doric or Lallans) is spoken by about 30 percent of the population, Gaelic by about 1 percent.

aqilokoq
noun
Inuktitut
ack-il-ok-yok

Meaning gently falling snow, initially noted down by an anthropologist traveling in northern Canada in the 1880s, who also misunderstood the sentence structure of the language and thus caused the widespread confusion around Inuit culture having or not having countless words for snow – *aqilokoq* is as much a phrase as it is a single word.

Both the Inuit (Inuktitut being one of the main Inuit languages) and Yupik language branches (within the Inuit-Yupik-Unangan language family) are polysynthetic – polysynthesis describes a language in which words can be made up of many morphemes, allowing a large amount of information to be contained within a complex, single word that functions as an entire sentence.

In Iñupiaq, spoken by the Iñupiat people of Northwestern Alaska, there is a word that means brushing snow from one's boots before entering a house, which demonstrates polysynthesis:

The word *tuluktuq* means to brush off snow before going inside, *tuluktuqtut* means they are brushing off snow from boots before going inside, and *Tuluktuġutin* is an instruction to do so. Other Iñupiaq terms related to snowiness:

qayuqłak, the rippled surface of snow

nutaġaq, fresh snow

qiqsruqqaq, glazed snow in thawing times

sitḷiq, hard snow with a crust

auksałak, melting snow

mauġaq, to wade through snow

Other snowy things:

flukkra, large-flaked gentle snow (Shetland)

hundslappadrífa, heavy snowfall in calm conditions, literally dog's-paw snow (Icelandic)

snaw-bree, melted snow (Scots)

peaux de lièvre, heavily falling snow, literally 'hare skins' (Quebecois)

glisk
noun
Scots
glisk

A word moving in meaning depending on its context, but describes something brief, a glimpse, a glance, a sense of something momentary and ephemeral, such as a fleeting slice of sun, or sunlight, as seen through a break in cloud.

die Füchse kochen Kaffee
phrase
German
dee FOOK-se KOCH-en KAF-ee

A regional German phrase for mist, literally translated as 'the foxes are making coffee,' and particularly referring to the kind of early morning mist that sits low and persistent in cold valleys.

pimashu
verb
Innu-aimun
pi-mah-HOH

To move with the wind.

kaajhuab
noun
Hmong
gah-oo-ab

Literally meaning 'light-fog' and describing morning light that dissolves a mist in a tonal language spoken by Hmong people in southern China and Southeast Asia, with over 2.7 million speakers of mainly mutually unintelligible varieties.

aiteall
noun
Irish
AT-chull

Describes a brief period of pleasant weather between two rain showers, though it can also be used to mean the idea of finding or paying attention to the beautiful pieces of life, even among all the difficult things.

冰雪 / bīngxuě
noun
Mandarin
bing-shoo-ay

Bīngxuě means 'ice and snow,' and is used when describing severe winter conditions, bringing with it images of snow-covered lands and the kind of peacefulness that only occurs when our worlds are covered in a deep cold.

初雪 / hatsuyuki
noun
Japanese
hah-tsoo-yoo-kee

A word specifically for the first snow of the year, formed of the kanji 初, meaning first or beginning, and 雪, meaning snow.

χελιδονιάς / chelidoniás

noun
Greek, Colloquial
CHEH-li-DOH-nas

Noted both in a Latin dictionary from 1879 and a French dictionary from 1934 as an old Greek weather term referring to 'swallow-bearing' winds, likely making its way into these dictionaries from a specific small region or even a village, as weather patterns have varying local names – in this case, warm spring winds coming from the west after 22 February, which converge with the return of swallows, assisting them on their spring migration north.

From the Ancient Greek χελιδών (*khelīdṓn*), meaning swallow, with the modern term for the bird being χελιδόνι (*chelidóni*).

brumal
adjective
English
BROO-muhl

Meaning of winter, belonging or pertaining to winter. From the Latin *bruma*, meaning winter and its shortest day.

The first known use of *brumal* was in 1522, within a translation by a poet-bishop who lived less than twenty miles from where I currently reside – it consequently feels as though I am a stone's throw from some kind of deep, original winter.

飓风 / jùfēng
noun
Mandarin
joo-fong

A hurricane, or cyclone. In traditional script written 颶風 with the above simplified script, and *jùfēng* being the romanization of the word in *Hanyu Pinyin* (pinyin literally means 'spelled sounds').

Mandarin (普通话) was developed as a formal, standardized language, based heavily on the Beijing dialect – being the preference of the communist party it used to be called 'official speech,' or 官话, and is also not mutually intelligible with Yue Chinese varieties, a fact that, along with active restriction of the latter, means the overall diversity of language has diminished.

خماسين / khamasīn
noun
Egyptian Arabic
kha-ma-SIN

A dry, hot and oppressive sand wind coming from the south of Egypt and across the Red Sea after the beginning of spring, usually arriving in late April or May, with an approximately fifty-day period during which the winds occur, perhaps two times per week. *Khamasīn* is a modern form of *khamsūn*, meaning fifty, and the wind is referred to as *rih al khamsin*, 'the wind of fifty days.' There are words from other languages and places in the world to mean similar types of wind:

aajej, a desert whirlwind (southern Morocco)

simoom, the sand wind sweeping across deserts in spring and summer, from the Arabic *semūm*, meaning 'to poison' (the Arabian Peninsula)

bād sad ve bist ruzeh, meaning 'wind of 120 days' (Iran and Afghanistan)

brickfielder, a wind from the Southern Australian desert

leveche, a warm wind in Spain ahead of low-pressure systems in the Sahara Desert; also called *sirocco* in some areas of the Mediterranean, which refers to the blisteringly hot sand winds of Northern Africa

sukhovey, a warm dust storm in the Gobi Desert of Mongolia

沃雨 / ag-hou
verb
Teochew
ack-houh

Meaning to be caught by rain, to get wet in the rain.

Teochew, from the Southern Min language group, is not mutually intelligible with Mandarin, Cantonese or Shanghainese, and contains within it many dialects of substantial difference, which means even the verb above would be pronounced very differently depending on where it is being spoken and used.

Chinese is not a language in and of itself but rather a writing system, such as Latin or Arabic, and 汉字 (*hànzì*, the characters of the writing system, are known as 唐人字, or *Dengnang-ji*, in Teochew) have been adopted by Vietnamese (chữ Hán), Korean (*hanja*), and Japanese (*kanji*). China's tapestry of dialects and languages, with vastly differing pronunciations, can all be written in Hanzi. That European languages use the Latin alphabet when written down but are pronounced so differently is a reasonably good analogy.

pirr
noun
Shetland
purr

A barely perceptible, gentle breeze. A light breath of wind can also be referred to as a *laar*.

breaclá
noun
Irish (Gaeilge)
BRACK-law

Meaning a dappled day; a day of mixed weather with sun and rain showers.

les bruixes es pentinen
phrase
Catalan
les BRU-shes es PAN-ti-nan

Literally translating as 'the witches comb their hair,' *les bruixes es pentinen* is a Catalan phrase referring to a sun-shower, a rain falling while the sun is still shining. Meanwhile in French, a sun-shower is called a *mariage de loup*, literally a 'wolf wedding.'

cnap-gaoithe

noun
Scottish Gaelic
knap GOOY-uh

Describing a very strong, gusty wind, a squall. *Cnap* can remarkably also mean the following: protrusion, small lumpy hill, thump, button and potato.

Home

Or: *The closest any of us
will ever get to the feeling*

I've had a lot of conversations with people about home – about what it is and isn't, whether it is a feeling or a verbal distinction or something altogether more guttural, about whether we can ever manage to adequately convey to another what the idea of home means to us, at its most personal. Home can be problematic and precise and vague and inexplicable and unbending and everywhere and no place at all and forgotten and missed and longed for. For the fortunate, it might be enmeshed with a pre-verbal feeling of physical safety, warm arms; for others, something finally scraped together by any means and against all odds. Whatever a person's first articulation of home is, whether that articulation is verbal or physical, nothing will ever quite shake it from the body.

We often conflate home with safety, and why shouldn't we, seeing how every person on this busy and finite planet deserves at the very least physical safety, water, warmth, nourishment and respect. How far we have to go, how little true attention is paid to the pain – if and when attention is paid to those who have had those basic rights removed from them, or prevented from ever obtaining them, that attention is only politicized and rehearsed and parroted, made meaningless by a two-faced lack of action, by blatant obfuscation. Home, then, is complicated where it shouldn't have to be, complicated by the fact that in some places home is wealth and object and status and excess, while in others it has been turned to dust and death by decisions made across oceans and borders. For millions of people to be so comfortable – at home – in oblivion and dismissal is horrifying, when home should and could at this point in time be found in an acceptance of differences and the unquestionable protection of those who have been left reeling from violence, from exploitation, from marginalization.

We conflate home with memory, too, blending those memories into something most recognizable as nostalgia, the textures and images of childhoods and previous selves tugging at us if we happen to be wearing something with long-enough sleeves. The feeling of something you couldn't bring with you as far as this present moment, of things that had to remain residing in the past no matter how much you wished otherwise. Childhood surroundings that shrink and often become disfigured with time, sometimes best not revisited, and the memories made before you became so aware of everything, of how fragile the notion of home can be.

Home can, really, be anything: a forest, a tiled floor, an island, a person. We are always trying and choosing to get back home, to a feeling or to places that, and people who, we've decided at one time or another fulfill enough of the criteria for home. This can look like being pulled back to places that were long ago left, abandoned or forsaken, possibly because we can feel more real in them than within the strangeness of elsewhere, but it can also look like leaving that which is most familiar and arriving somewhere foreign that feels more like home than ever seemed conceivable. If home is ever constructed from memory, then it can also be choosing to forget.

Home is also found in taking care, in lighting a fire, in a grandfather slowly washing dishes after dinner, in routine, in environmental rhythms, and in hoping that all we love isn't taken from us too quickly. Home might in fact be listening to a loved one's heart beating in the middle of the night if only because you know it cannot last forever.

You can build a home or you can believe in home or you can break a home or you can do away with it once and for all. But inherently it becomes that which you know more intricately than anything else, the corners of it both cobwebbed and committed to memory. You can stray from home, find your way back, and ask for someone to stay there with you. It can be filled with noise or silence, with food, with fastidiousness, with fear. There isn't a single definition of home, and this might be why it's possible to both find it in so many places and also confine it to one.

Whatever your feelings or thoughts on home, it is clear there needs to be a general consensus when it comes to recognizing that one of our shared homes, our home planet, has been made sick, and that taking responsibility for actionably healing it must now be a part of this life. An important part of the here and now, because it might not be an option in the later. Language can build us a home, language is acutely necessary to better understand and protect our collective one, and the following words will help with that, whether you are missing home or already there, if you don't yet have a definition for home or wish for one, if you feel that you've lost home, if you already suspect exactly where it resides in the body, if you like to leave a light on.

maadoittuminen
verbal noun
Finnish
MAAH-doy-too-mi-nen

Describing the act of rooting oneself in nature, finding connection to and with the natural world. Coming from the transitive verb *maadoittaa*, which in the context of electricity literally means 'earthing' or 'grounding.'

居場所 / ibasho

noun
Japanese
ee-bah-shoh

A dictionary might translate *ibasho* as whereabouts, or location, but in a deeper way, it means a place where a person belongs, feels at home, often in relation to both mental and physical wellbeing, and in recent years the term has been increasingly used within Japanese social services and education to describe inclusive spaces for those most vulnerable. A place to live safely and well, with dignity and real connection – basic human things that all people deserve. The word ibasho is formed from the verb *iru*, which means to exist, and *basho*, which means place.

cynefin
noun
Welsh
kuh-NEV-een

Meaning haunt or habitat, *cynefin* carries a sense of rootedness along with all of those overlapping factors of environment and experience accompanying the place where a person was born, or feels at home in. Somewhere we can feel a sense of belonging and familiarity.

An earlier usage of cynefin was by Welsh sheep farmers, describing how their animals would naturally find and graze a certain naturally defined area within the landscape.

Fernweh

noun
German
FERN-vee

Literally translating as 'far-pain,' *Fernweh* means a kind of sickness for the far away, a longing for distant places – an inverse of sorts to homesickness, for which the German is *Heimweh* – and can also denote a wishing for an alternative way of life.

solastalgia

noun
English, New Coinage
SOH-las-TAHL-juh

Describes the distress that comes from witnessing degradation of the environment, one's home, through things such as drought, mountaintop removal, fossil fuel extraction, oil spills, a general or specific climatic falling-apart. A homesickness while already *being* home, the pain from seeing one's environment altered and destroyed, rendered unrecognizable. Coined by Australian philosopher Glenn Albrecht over twenty years ago.

tūrangawaewae

noun
Māori
too-RUNG-uh-WAY-way

The place in Māori culture where a person is rooted and connected, by kinship and belonging, somewhere the person has a right to exist. Often translated as 'a place to stand,' it connotes independence and identity, formed from the words *tūranga* (standing place) and *waewae* (feet).

focolare

noun
Italian
foh-koh-LAH-reh

Literally meaning hearth, or fireplace, *focolare*, as a physical or emotional centre, is also used to mean 'home' – to return to one's home is *tornare al proprio focolare*.

Wahlheimat

noun
German
VAHL-hi-mat

A *Wahlheimat* is an adopted country, place or home, literally meaning 'choice-home.'

عَصَبِيّة / aṣabiyya

noun
Arabic
aa-sa-BEY-ya

Aṣabiyya refers to a 'group feeling,' a social connectedness and solidarity stemming from kinship, or from ideologies, a shared purpose. It is derived from the root عصب (*asab*), meaning encompassing or holding.

Gemütlichkeit

noun
German
geh-MOOT-lich-kite

A cornerstone German concept, *Gemütlichkeit* is a kind of opposite to stress of many kinds. A warmth, a friendliness, a feeling of comfort and home, but one that layers both the physical and the emotional. The adjective form, *gemütlich*, comes from the word *Gemüt*, which simply means mood or disposition.

Things can also be described as *ungemütlich*, which might be something like feeling uncomfortably hot, or the lights being far too bright.

የተውልድ አገር / yetwld ager
noun
Amharic
YE-twled a-ger

Literally meaning 'birth country' and referring to a homeland, home place, native country, another word for homeland being እናት አገር (enat hager).

Amharic, one of the Southern Semitic languages and the most widely spoken (of more than eighty) in Ethiopia, is now believed to be even older than Northern Semitic languages such as Hebrew and Arabic. In addition to Amharic, the other official languages of Ethiopia are Afar, Omoro, Somali and Tigrinya.

The last of these languages, Tigrinya, is spoken in both Eritrea and the northernmost region of Ethiopia, Tigray, a place that has for years been suffering extreme violence, with the Tigrayan people ongoingly targeted as an ethnic group by the Ethiopian government, including between the years 2020 and 2022, when 600,000 people died amid violence and forced starvation.

χώρος / chóros
noun
Greek
KORR-os

Used to describe literal space, such as a place or a room, but can also describe an abstract area or domain.

cwtch
noun
Welsh
kutch

The safest kind of embrace or hug, containing a sense of home and real emotional significance. Something a person might yearn for during times of fear or stress, a *cwtch* contains within it the magic of being alive and therefore being able to love. Sometimes written as *cwtsh*.

querencia
noun
Spanish
keh-REHN-si-yah

A kind of homing instinct, the pull one feels to a place, somewhere that draws you back to it and where you feel secure and safe. It isn't so much a nostalgia or a bittersweet longing (*añoranza*, the Spanish equivalent of the Portuguese *saudade*), or even a homesickness, but a place can be your *querencia*, or you can feel querencia toward somewhere or someone, a sort of deep affection or emotional inclining toward a location or person.

Different from *terruño*, which is the place where a person is born, a native soil and terrain, though it is often used with emotion or nostalgia attached.

νόστος / nóstos

noun
Greek
NOHS-tohs

In Ancient Greek mythology and literature, νόστος was the returning home of a hero from an epic journey of some sort, notably in Homer's *Odyssey*, with the word now rarely used in Modern Greek aside from in literary contexts – though its meaning, both as the act of reaching a place and of returning or going back, seems relevant still.

støvfnug
noun
Danish
STE-oof-nug

The Danish word *fnug* refers to a small quantity of something airborne, and *støvfnug* are the dust motes visible in bright, streaming sunlight, the kind of dust-light only noticed infrequently on slow, aimless afternoons at home.

Other small quantities: snowflakes are known as *snefnug*, and dandelion seeds are *mælkebøttefnug*. Fnug can also mean something small and easily overlooked, not necessarily literally but more figuratively.

morriña

noun
Galician
moh-RREE-nyah

A melancholia felt when far from home, a deeper and more complex sort of homesickness, an aching feeling directed toward a lost homeland or a faraway, unreachable place. As a word, it speaks to the strength of Galician culture and the region's long history of emigration.

peiskos
noun
Norwegian
PAISS-koos

Translated as something like 'fireplace coziness,' *peiskos* is formed from the words *peis*, meaning fireplace, and *kos*, meaning cozy, or hug. Its full meaning is the feeling obtained by sitting in front of a warm fire, an event in and of itself.

The best kind of night for peiskos might well be *stjerneklart*, when a night is dark, quiet and accompanied solely by stars.

φιλοξενία / filoxenía
noun
Greek
fee-LOHK-sen-ni-ah

Literally translating as 'stranger-friend,' *filoxenía*, from φίλος (*fílos*) meaning friend and ξένος (*xénos*) meaning stranger, is the love and kindness shown to strangers or guests as a genuine, open and friendly hospitality, though inferring more emotion and a deeper desire for connection than our English term 'hospitality' does.

mysig
adjective
Swedish
mee-SIG

Used to describe something that affords warmth and comfort, such as curling up in a comfortable chair in the evening, or remaining under a blanket on the coldest winter days – very much associated with home or friendly gatherings. Can be a verb as *att mysa*.

Being

Or: *The brief condition of it,
and how incredible it is to have thoughts at all*

Some days – slightly too many lately – it doesn't feel as though humans are, overall, making a very positive attempt at *being*. It is a brief condition, and yet the infinitesimal lifetime of a single person can still be filled by incomprehensible violence and oppression, whether that person is choosing to inflict those violences upon others or as the someone with a life being subjected to horrors. We could *be* a lot nicer to each other. You might think of humans as the unbearably overconfident member of a mixed group, dripping in monetary wealth and apparent social value and brashness and explanations and the certainty that everyone else wishes to be like them when, in fact, they are regarded by others in the group as overbearing, unfortunate and pitiable. I think this sometimes, that our neighbour species must look at us with this pity.

How exactly should a person be when freedom of speech seems less and less free, when books and histories and truths are banned from schools, when a living wage isn't remotely enough to live on, when basic health care costs more than most can afford, when bodily autonomy for many is slipping further away? How exactly should a person be when it is seemingly made impossible to reasonably and softly be a person?

One answer is presumably to just carry on despite, as gently as might be possible, pointing out the places in which people are suffering and in which things have been done badly, and badly done, and could be made much better. It is hard to discern sometimes what being should look like when surrounded by so many lasting-forever objects, so many constructions, so much that our ancient brain structures really cannot comprehend. Like when the legs can be running so quickly that the rest of the body cannot keep up, or like how you can never reach the horizon.

We are not always afforded very much time to be. Our tiny personal fractions of ordinary and beautiful being are vulnerable to infection and dictatorships and sea level rise, and this suits the designs of some people perfectly. For if we only ever have just enough time to survive, to scrape forward, and if being fully human becomes the exception, then it is very difficult to ever have a critical mass of sentiment and solidarity and demand for things to be made better. We have, it seems, been surrounded so entirely with windows and vehicles and sidewalks and systems to abide by that it has become quite difficult to see for any distance out of it. Difficult for us to see by design. If the time has been taken to figure out that the smallest black holes might measure ten to twenty times smaller than the size of a proton, then you would be forgiven for thinking that the time could also be put aside to figure out how to live on the planet in a way that doesn't brutally damage its health or the health of its inhabitants. I've always, always felt uneasy when reading news headlines about space travel – surely people shouldn't have the nerve to go and damage anything else before we've even mended things here?

When I think about how a person might be amid all of this, I think of how essential it is to keep even sand-grain-sized parts of yourself gently folded and protected, hidden away from the insistence and implementation of archaic and dangerous notions about productivity and pessimism and power. At the very least some sand-grain-sized parts that can still choose to feel the passing of the seasons and the pull of weather, feel time existing only as an interplay between light and dark, feel the pure unblinking astonishment of being here and breathing at all.

Parts that can perhaps remember the following: that there are white storks standing motionless at the edge of wetlands, that there is always someone who needs you to say a kind word in their direction, that plants drink the sun and that we would be nothing without them, that there are already enough items of clothing on the Earth for six more generations of people, that it's okay if you don't believe in precisely the same things as your neighbour and that respecting cultural difference is a very bare minimum, that the early morning blue of deepest winter can sometimes be physically uncomfortable, that we've likely lost as much knowledge as we've gained, that the oceans used to be heavy with slippery creatures and empty of plastic, and that all this really and truly is the briefest of conditions.

Some of the gentler ideas-for-being that follow in this chapter have intentionally been made difficult for us to live by, to embark upon, but they can be read as seeds of practices that could be chosen, prioritized, nurtured, offered up to others. These words are only a handful, but a handful nonetheless, a hand that suggests and imagines a near future in which we are less unbalanced, less frantic, less furious, less fearful. Where instead of truths being denied, they are acknowledged, where brokenness is mended, where life can altogether become a much more bearable condition for everybody.

Erlebnis
noun
German
air-LEEB-niss

A philosophical term translated as 'experience,' *Erlebnis* is experiencing life deeply, fully and within the present moment.

浮世 / ukiyo

noun
Japanese
oo-ki-yoh

Commonly translated now as 'floating world,' *ukiyo* was originally a Heian-period Buddhist term (憂き世) meaning 'the world of sorrow and grief,' describing the melancholic, ephemeral nature of existence. Later, in the culturally flourishing Edo or Tokugawa period (1603–1868), ukiyo was adopted by writers and artists to comment on that same fleetingness of life, with the implication being that time should be enjoyed while it (minimally) lasts, a shift in meaning toward the positive largely attributed to the writer and Shin Buddhist priest Asai Ryōi (浅井了意) and his 1661 prose collection titled *Ukiyo Monogatari*, 'Tales of the Floating World.' Now, ukiyo appears primarily in poetic, artistic, academic or historical contexts, rather than being a word actively used in daily life to reflect on the maybe-meanings of everything.

мѐрāк / merak
noun
Serbo-Croatian
MEH-rack

Мѐрāк is the pleasure derived from the smaller moments of life, the enjoyment of them, the paying attention to them, and a sense of kinship and connection with the universe as a result. Borrowed from the Ottoman Turkish مراق (*merak*), which primarily means curiosity.

It is the actively sought feeling derived from smaller, and often simple, short-term pleasures, which, in turn, lends itself to a feeling of fulfillment, connectedness and the appreciation of one's natural state of being. An example of мѐрāк might even be the Serbo-Croatian прȍмаја (*prȍmaja*), which refers to the wind felt on the body when standing between two open windows.

根回し / nemawashi

noun
Japanese
neh-mah-wah-shee

Used mainly in workplace contexts, though it comes from gardening, to mean going around the roots of something in advance of planting, for instance, if moving a tree into different or new soil, and so used within business to describe the process of building support and laying foundations, as for a project.

allemannsretten

noun
Norwegian
ALL-uh-mahns-rret-en

Literally meaning 'every person's right,' *allemannsretten* is a law in Norway, passed in 1957, that allows everyone to walk and roam freely on uncultivated land (*utmark*) – with certain caveats and exceptions – something that also exists in various iterations in Iceland, Sweden, Finland, Austria, Belarus, Scotland, Latvia, Lithuania, Switzerland and the Czech Republic.

friluftsliv

noun
Norwegian
free-LOOFTS-leev

Embodying the general love for nature in Norway, *friluftsliv* literally means 'free-air-life' and describes a way of being that comes from living in harmony with nature rather than trampling through and destroying it, as has long been the case in so many places in the world. Friluftsliv doesn't have much to do with expensive equipment or strenuous activities, rather it could simply be sitting in a local park and observing, or helping to ensure accessibility within nature, or taking the leafy paths slightly less traveled.

First recorded in written form in an 1863 poem – 'På vidderne,' meaning 'on the heights' – by Norwegian playwright Henrik Johan Ibsen: 'friluftsliv for mine tanker' ('outdoor life for my thoughts').

skogluft
noun
Norwegian
skorg-LOOFT

Translating as 'forest air,' *skogluft* describes the practice and philosophy of bringing nature inside into one's home, perhaps cuttings from a tree in the garden, or seasonal blooms, even the cultivation and care of indoor plants.

Weltschmerz
noun
German, New Coinage
VELT-schmertz

Literally meaning 'world-pain,' *Weltschmerz*, coined by a German author in 1827, describes a psychological world tiredness or weariness, sometimes a melancholy without particular origin, or a despair at the state of worldly happenings. Not necessarily a useful or productive kind of despair and defined more by apathy than action.

koyaanisqatsi

noun
Hopi
KOY-ah-niss-KAHT-see

Meaning a life out of balance, a life in turmoil, and literally 'chaotic life,' *koyaanisqatsi* is a word that calls for other ways of being in the world. It supposes that everything thought of as 'normal' is in fact abnormal, and comes from the Native American language spoken by the Hopi people of northeastern Arizona. Hopi holds a unique way of expressing concepts of time and space, of experiencing time – for instance, events that happen to a person a great physical distance away are talked about as if occurring in the distant past.

Koyaanisqatsi is also the title of a dialogue-free film from 1982, a time-lapse of cities and natural landscapes, and this quote from Philip Glass, who composed the score for the film, puts one of the sentiments that accompanies koyaanisqatsi succinctly:

> 'There seems to be no ability to see beyond, to see that we have encased ourselves in an artificial environment that has remarkably replaced the original, nature itself. We do not live with nature any longer.'

ᐃᓄᖃᑎᒌᑦᓯᐊᕐᓂᖅ / Inuuqatigiitsiarniq

phrase
Inuktitut
ee-nu-oo-kah-tee-geet-see-urh-nik

Describes being respectful of all people, health within communities and relationships, and caring for others; generally living peacefully.

ᐊᕙᑦᑎᓐᓂᒃ ᑲᒪᑦᓯᐊᕐᓂᖅ / Avatittinnik Kamatsiarniq

phrase
Inuktitut
ah-vah-tee-nik kamat-see-urh-nik

Care for and stewardship of the environment, respect for land, for animals – for everything that is alive and part of ecosystems. As with *Inuuqatigiitsiarniq*, this is a part of Inuit Qaujimajatuqangit, a body of traditional Inuit knowledge and values, translated literally to mean 'that which has long been known by Inuit.'

In a short 2022 documentary about *Avatittinnik Kamatsiarniq* and climate change, an Inuit elder speaks to the camera of the changes he noticed in the surrounding environment, describing how people used to feel glad on the rare occasion when a ship arrived to the area bringing much-needed supplies, that now it is very different:

> 'When there is a ship passing by, I feel sadness. I watch whales up there through binoculars and my eyes.'

He describes how the whales will try to move out of a ship's path, both as the ships arrive and leave, that they never see whales just calmly existing in the water anymore – not coming up to the water's surface to greet each other with their tusks, not bearing young.

無常 / mujō

noun
Japanese
mu-joh

Originating in Buddhism alongside 苦 (*ku*, or suffering) and 無我 (*muga*, or non-self) as one of the 三法印 (*sanbōin*, or Three Marks of Existence), *mujō* is impermanence, the knowledge that there is no such thing as absolute, or certainty, that everything is ultimately ephemeral and in a continual state of change and becoming.

sisu
noun
Finnish
SEE-so

Though other languages have comparable concepts, *sisu* is uniquely Finnish, a particular sort of grit, courage and perseverance, which as an idea stretches back hundreds of years. Coming from the root word *sisä-*, meaning inner, sisu means resilience and tenacity, is action-oriented, and often found in the context of harsh conditions, whether elemental, geographical or mental.

In other languages, comparable ideas are 頑張る (*ganbaru*) in Japanese, *seny* in Catalan, and the Palestinian steadfastness of صمود (*ṣumūd*), which is deeply connected to the experience of violent and long-term displacement and oppression, a concept closely related to land and Indigenousness, becoming an even more prominent cultural value following the 1967 Naksa and, as both 'static' ṣumūd and 'resistance' ṣumūd (*ṣumūd muqāwim*), remains a hugely meaningful part of the ongoing Palestinian fight for self-determination, the right to exist.

Imasuugtua

phrase
Sugpiaq
im-ah-shook-too-ah

Imasuugtua means to be sad, or downhearted, or having a sinking feeling, but its literal translation is 'to be searching for one's contents.' From the word *imaq*, meaning sea or ocean, but also contents and 'a liquid contained inside.'

Sugpiaq (also called Alutiiq or Sugcestun) has two major dialects and is a close relative of the Central Alaskan Yup'ik language. Traditionally, the people refer to themselves as Sugpiaq (*suk* meaning person and *-piaq* meaning real, the plural being Sugpiat), with Alutiiq coming from a term used by Russian colonizers (1794–1867) who preceded the American ones (1867–present).

σιγά σιγά / sigá sigá
interjection
Greek
SI-gah SI-gah

Meaning slowly, or slowly but surely, a kind of unhurriedness, with the expression having an endless array of situations and moments in, and to, which it can be applied.

Particularly delightful is the Greek idiom σιγά τα λάχανα (*sigá ta láchana*), literally translating as 'slow down, it's just cabbage,' and meaning something is not *that* important, or at least not as important as it is made out to be.

κοσμοπολίτης / kosmopolítis
noun
Greek
KOS-moh-poh-lee-tis

As the origin of the word 'cosmopolitan,' κοσμοπολίτης initially meant a world citizen – κόσμος (*kósmos*) meaning world or universe, and πολίτης (*polítis*) meaning citizen – a citizen not only of the planet underfoot but of the cosmos and the universe, as the word κόσμος did not only mean world as in globe but world as in *everything*, the complete natural order of things.

In modern Greek usage, it describes a person who has seen many pieces and many cultures of the planet, who has traveled through and witnessed or lived within them, a discerning wanderer.

静寂 / seijaku

noun
Japanese
sei-jah-koo

One of the seven aesthetic Zen principles within Japanese design, *seijaku* references a stillness that allows for a contemplative state of mind, a quietude, as atmosphere created in which a person can be invited toward an internal calm, within an environment or landscape – calmness nestled within the chaos of life. Formed from *sei* (静, quiet) and *jaku* (寂, tranquility).

mokita
noun
Kilivila
moh-KEE-tah

In Kilivila, spoken on the Trobriand Islands of Papua New Guinea, *mokita* holds the precise meaning of 'a truth known by everyone but not discussed or spoken about,' though it might, of course, be discussed anyway. Also commonly expressed as *mokwita*, and less commonly as *monita*.

айляк / ailyak
noun
Bulgarian
ai-LYAK

Describes the practice of not rushing through life, of doing things slowly and savouringly, of enjoying the process. A sibling of sentimental sorts to the Swahili phrase *hakuna matata*.

मुदिता / muditā

noun
Pāli, Sanskrit
MUH-di-tah

The sympathetic or vicarious pleasure and joy that is found in the wellbeing or happiness of others, in others doing well, a sort of choice to lean toward joy no matter the circumstances. A feeling completely unconcerned with self-interest – an antonym to jealousy or envy.

тэгш / tegš

noun
Mongolian
TEH-gsh

The state of being in balance and harmony with both one's community and the wider world.

iwígara

noun
Tarahumara (Rarámuri ra'ícha)
ih-WEE-gah-ra

A belief of the Indigenous Rarámuri people of Northern Mexico, *iwígara* means 'shared breath' and refers to the interconnectedness of all things, both physically and spiritually.

sankofa

noun
Akan Twi
SAHN-koh-fa

Literally translating as something like 'to retrieve,' *sankofa* comes from the Ghanaian Akan tribe and, as a concept, expresses the need to look back at the past in order to better understand our present, to imagine and live a better future. The Bono Adinkra symbol for sankofa (Adinkra are Ghanaian symbols used to represent concepts and ideas) depicts a bird with its head turned back toward an egg, representing past knowledge that can inform a more beautiful future.

기분 / gibun
noun
Korean
ki-buhn

Often literally translated as 'mood,' 기분 (*gibun*) refers to an individual's emotional state of being, and as such, it is seen as important to respect the gibun of others, something valued in a matter-of-fact, neutral way in the context of interpersonal relationships.

hleów-feðer
noun
Old English
HLAY-oh-feth-er

A sheltering wing or arm, literally meaning 'shelter-feather,' meaning an arm placed protectively around another, the keeping safe of another, standing in such a way as to absorb the strength of a wind.

víðsýni

noun
Icelandic
VEETH-see-ni

A compound word formed of *víður* (wide) and *sýni* (vision), *víðsýni* refers to a literal panoramic, expansive view, and also to a state of liberal open-mindedness.

ευδαιμονία / evdaimonía

noun
Greek
ev-de-mo-NI-ah

Translated as something like 'welfare' or 'human flourishing,' *eudaimonia* in Ancient Greek literature was written about as the highest form of human goodness and happiness, literally ευ (*ef*) meaning good and δαίμων (*daímōn*) meaning spirit or deity – a contented prosperity that is not a means to an end or an ephemeral state but rather a generally desired way of being.

kaukokaipuu
noun
Finnish
KAU-koh-kai-poh

Literally 'faraway yearning,' and similar but different from wanderlust (in Finnish wanderlust is translated as *vaellushalu*), *kaukokaipuu* is a compound word naming the impulse or longing to travel to distant places, though it can also be a kind of homesickness for places as yet unvisited and unseen.

Has similarities with the Welsh *hiraeth* and the German *Sehnsucht*.

כואב לי הלב / koev li halev
expression
Hebrew
koh-EHV lee ha-LEHV

Translating as something like an 'aching heart,' *koev li halev* is a deep empathy, identifying with the suffering of other somethings, or other someones, such that you can feel their pain in your own body.

소확행 / sohwakhaeng

noun
Korean
soh-wak-haeng

A small but distinct happiness or comfort, such as putting one's face into laundry just out of the dryer – rather than an intense or overwhelming feeling, *sohwakhaeng* is a small nugget of something good.

Sohwakhaeng is an abbreviated form of the phrase 소소하지만 확실한 행복 (*sosohajiman hwaksilhan haengbok*), which, if taken piece by piece, means small or trivial (sosohajiman), certain or definite (hwaksilhan), and then haengbok, a noun referring to a state of emotional satisfaction or joy. Sohwakhaeng is therefore understood to mean a minimal unit of happiness.

tuko pamoja
expression
Swahili
too-koh pah-moh-ja

Literally meaning 'one place,' *tuko pamoja* expresses a shared sense of purpose, feeling and motivation within a group or community, something that stretches beyond concurrence to a compassionate understanding. It can be used to express solidarity, excitement or even as a question in some contexts, and though the extremely broad nature of its application could appear as dilution, this is not the case, and, really, we could do with far more ways to say: One togetherness, that's all we get.

nepakartojama
adjective
Lithuanian
NEP-ah-KARR-tor-yama

Translating into English as 'unrepeatable,' *nepakartojama* describes a situation so subjectively beautiful and perfect that it could not possibly ever happen again.

scatenarsi
verb
Italian
scah-teh-NAR-si

To run wild, to break free, to run amok.

Coming from *catena*, meaning chain, this connotes freeing something from somewhere. You can *scaternare* an emotion, and strong weather phenomena can also *scatenarsi* themselves – releasing the powers of wind and rain and rage in the direction of change for the better, change for the more beautiful.

'If you are not sure what you think about something, the most useful questions are these: Are you being kind? Are they being kind? That usually gives you the answer.'

– Jan Morris

Acknowledgements

Words to Love a Planet has been helped and held by a lot of thoughtful hands, and my thanks encompass not only the person who first said *yes!* at Andrews McMeel, the singular Patty Rice; the book's technically second editor but best understander, Melissa Rhodes Zahorsky; its designers, Tiffany Meairs and Diane Marsh; its production manager, Tamara Haus; its production editor, Kayla Overbey, and linguistic support, Dayten Rose; its beady-eyed copyeditor, Amy Strassner, and proofreader, Rima Weinberg; its main marketing and publicity advocate, Kat Anstine; and my ever-hard-working US and UK agents, Jennifer Weltz and Holly Faulks, but also (and hugely) the native speakers, heritage speakers and translators who generously agreed to read through my offerings and where necessary add the kind of deep nuance that can only come from someone who has a belonging to the language, or languages, in question: Eugénie and Mohamed Abdalmoaty, Joe Aparna, Begum Ayfer, Jagadish Babu, Leena Balme, Aida E. Bedri, Chrissy Beisly, Catrine Bollerslev, Zhui Ning Chang, Hannah Ní Dhoimhín, Áine Uí Dhonnghaile, Dr. Linus Digm'rina, Mira Droumeva, Kristina Fujikake, Laurie Goodlad, Dauvit Horsbroch, Mita Kapur, Tan Siok Kia, Mojca Kristan, Colin Lie, Alma Liezenga, Paulina Machnik, Calum Maclean, Joanna Marcus, Niklas Mey, Jerome Mayaud, 林名瀚, Dhruvi Modi, Maru de Montserrat, Prof. Dorcas Obiri-Yeboah, Mila Peršić, Nada Peršić, Vuk Peršić, Christina Pikhmanets, Teresa Poeta, Tomos Prys-Jones, Mac Ramsay, Adam Sandström, Sreeyuktha S, David Sumner, Angeline Swee, Sarah Sypris, Ásta Thoroddsen, Loukas Tsouknidas, Dr. Viveka Velupillai, Huiqi Wang, Ben White and Tatjana Zoldnere.

I'm grateful that this UK edition was embraced by the expertise and patience of those at Michael O'Mara Books, with huge appreciation for the careful time spent on its outside and inside by senior commissioning editor Nell Warner, proofreader Vincent Camacho and designer Natasha Le Coultre.

Thank you to my close and closest humans for giving me their time and their love and their listening as I worked on this book – I'm not sure anyone ever needs more than that when those things are done well.

And thank you, too, if you're reading this, all the way to the end.

Index of Terms

A
aajej, 159
aarniometsä, 65
Abendrot, 84
ag-hou (沃雨), 160
ailyak (айляк), 212
aiteall, 154
al-Ghasaq (الغَسَق), 89
allemannsretten, 198
allhvass, 145
amhdhorchacht, 89
amipushu, 105
ammil, 121
amurg, 88
anaamiindim, 133
andvari, 145
apricity, 4
aqilokoq, 150
aranyhíd, 112
aşabiyya, (عَصَبِيَّة), 176
auksałak, 151
Avatittinnik Kamatsiarniq (ᐊᕙᑏᑦᓂᒃ ᑲᒪᑦᓯᐊᕐᓂᖅ), 205

B
bād sad ve bist ruzeh, 159
Bergdenken, 49
bīngxuě (冰雪), 155
Blueschtfährtli, 19
bon hiver, 15
breaclá, 161
brickfielder, 159
brontide, 148
brumal, 157
bürenkhii (бүрэнхий), 88

C
camhanaich, 87
cāral (சாரல்), 122
celístia, 59
chandamama (చందమామ), 92
chelidoniás (χελιδονιάς), 156
chóros (χώρος), 180
chrysalism, 111
cnap-gaoithe, 162
controra, 83
crepúsculo, 88
curglaff, 105
cwtch, 181
cyfnos, 88
cynefin, 170

D
desir, 56
die Füchse kochen Kaffee, 152
dreich, 149
dúnalogn, 145

E
earthshine, 70
erämaajärvi, 130
Erlebnis, 194
estivation, 18
evdaimonía (ευδαιμονία), 219

F
fárviðri, 145
fellibylur, 145
Fernweh, 171
fiidkii, 89
filoxenía (φιλοξενία), 188
fjellvant, 49
flukkra, 151
focolare, 175
friluftsliv, 199
Frischluftfanatiker, 140
frondescence, 16
Frühjahrsmüdigkeit, 146

Index of Terms

fūbutsushi (風物詩), 30
fukinsei (不均斉), 43

G

Gemütlichkeit, 177
gibun (기분), 216
glas, 66
glisk, 152
gluggaveður, 144
godhuli (गोधूलि), 89
gökotta, 78
gola, 145
graupel, 139
grimlins, 85
gully washer, 123

H

hanami (花見), 14
hanyauku, 42
hatsuyuki (初雪), 155
heavengravel, 138
hleów-feðer, 217
hnjúkapeyr, 145
hundslappadrífa, 151
huya ania, 50
hvass, 145
hvassviðri, 145
hwanghon (황혼), 88
hyetal, 123

I

ibasho (居場所), 169
ilunabarra, 89
Imasuugtua, 208
Inuuqatigiitsiarniq (ᐃᓄᖃᑎᒌᑦᓯᐊᕐᓂᖅ), 204–5
iwígara, 214

J

jùfēng (颶风), 158

K

kaajhuab, 153
kaamos, 34
kahkašân (کهکشان), 60
kaldi, 145
kaukokaipuu, 220
kawaakari (川明かり), 117
kertik, 57
khamasīn (خماسين), 159
kłúsx̌nítkʷ, 116
kō (候), 20
koev li halev (כואב לי הלב), 221
koko, 125
kosmopolítis (κοσμοπολίτης), 210
koyaanisqatsi, 202–3
kōyō (紅葉), 11
krēsla, 89
kuāua, 125
kul, 145

L

lacuna, 119
laethanta na riabhaí, 23
léishēng dà, yǔdiǎn xiǎo (雷声大，雨点小), 128
les bruixes es pentinen, 161
leveche, 159
lieko, 54
linnunmaito, 131
listopad (листопад), 11
luscofusco, 95

M

maadoittuminen, 168
maalai (மாலை), 89
madrugada, 77
madwebiisaa, 107
Maeinschein, 12
magharibi, 88
mäntykangas, 58
manvasanai (மண்வாசனை), 110
marcescence, 28
mareel, 114
mauġaq, 151
merak (мѐрāк), 196
meriggiare, 82
mokita, 212
montivagant, 48
morriña, 186
muditā (मुदिता), 213
muḥīṭ (محيط), 106
mujō (無常), 206
mysig, 189

N

nagisa (渚), 104
namir (نمير), 127
nāulu, 124
nemawashi (根回し), 197
nepakartojama, 224
nóstos (νόστος), 184
nutaġaq, 151

O

offing, 118
oogly, 140
ortzimuga, 71
ótta, 96

Index of Terms

P

passeggiata, 51–2
peaux de lièvre, 151
peiskos, 187
petrichor, 108–10
pimashu, 153
pirr, 161
plenilune, 92
pogodnie, 147
Poʻonui, 125
potamichor, 109
psithurism, 13

Q

qayuqłak, 151
qiqsruqqaq, 151
querencia, 181

R

resolana, 141
ritornello, 45
rummescent, 12

S

salicetum, 67
sandfok, 145
sankofa, 215
scatenarsi, 225
seijaku (静寂), 211
serein, 122
shafaq (شفق), 88
shinrin-yoku (森林浴), 27
shinryoku (新緑), 24
shom, 88
sigásigá (σιγά σιγά), 209
simoom, 159
sisu, 207
sitḷiq, 151
skafrenningur, 145
skogluft, 200
skovstilhed, 46
skúmaskot, 97
smultronställe, 64
snaw-bree, 151
snicket, 44
sohwakhaeng (소확행), 222
sólarfrí, 147
solastalgia, 38, 172
sōlstitium, 22
solvegg, 5
soodraght, 132
stinningskaldi, 145
støvfnug, 185
ṣubḥ kādib (صُبْح كاذب), 81
sukhovey, 159
sunnablær, 145
sūryāstamayaṁ (സൂര്യാസ്തമയം), 84
sutemos, 86
sutinky (сутінки), 89
súton, 86
sviptivindar, 145

T

takatalvi, 32
tegš (тэгш), 214
tharurru, 98
trasnochar, 94
tsukimi (月見), 91
tuko pamoja, 223
tuḷir (துளிர்), 29
tuluktuq, 151
tunglmyrkvi, 93
turadh, 143
tūrangawaewae, 174
tweavelet, 120

U

uashtessiu, 10
úht-cearu, 76
uitwaaien, 53
ukiyo (浮世), 195
utu (उत्), 8
utu, 129

V

vedriti, 127
víðsýni, 218
viriditas, 55
volia (воля), 63
vólta (βόλτα), 52
výrij (вирій), 17

W

Waʻahila, 125
Wahlheimat, 176
Waldsterben, 68
Wari, 6
Weltschmerz, 201
winterċeariġ, 31

X

xiá (霞), 80

Y

yakamoz, 113
yaldâ (يلدا), 33
yetwld ager (የተውልድ አገር), 178
yillal, 40

Z

zastruga (заструга), 126
zeg (ዘጋ), 90
Zeitgeber, 9
zirimiri, 142

About the Author

Ella Frances Sanders is a *New York Times* and internationally bestselling author and illustrator of six books variously about languages, science and beauty. In addition to making books, she is the designer for *Orion* magazine and writes a column about words within its pages called 'Root Catalog.' She lives in a small town in a river valley lying just into the Highlands of Scotland.

First published in Great Britain in 2026 by
Michael O'Mara Books Limited
9 Lion Yard
Tremadoc Road
London SW4 7NQ

EU representative:
Authorised Rep Compliance Ltd
Ground Floor, 71 Baggot Street Lower
Dublin D02 P593
Ireland

Copyright © Ella Frances Sanders 2026

All rights reserved. You may not copy, store, distribute, transmit, reproduce or otherwise make available this publication (or any part of it) in any form, or by any means (electronic, digital, optical, mechanical, photocopying, recording, machine readable, text/data mining or otherwise), without the prior written permission of the publisher. Any person who does any unauthorized act in relation to this publication may be liable to criminal prosecution and civil claims for damages.

A CIP catalogue record for this book is available from the British Library.

This product is made of material from well-managed, FSC®-certified forests and other controlled sources. The manufacturing processes conform to the environmental regulations of the country of origin.

For further information see www.mombooks.com/about/sustainability-climate-focus
Report any safety issues to product.safety@mombooks.com and see
www.mombooks.com/contact/product-safety

UK edition:
ISBN: 978-1-78929-900-7 in hardback print format

1 2 3 4 5 6 7 8 9 10

Printed and bound in China

www.mombooks.com